Sharing Our Faith

LOVING OTHERS THROUGH EVANGELISM

KRISTYN PEREZ

Study Suggestions

We believe that the Bible is true, trustworthy, and timeless and that it is vitally important for all believers. These study suggestions are intended to help you more effectively study Scripture as you seek to know and love God through His Word.

SUGGESTED STUDY TOOLS

A Bible

A double-spaced, printed copy of the Scripture passages that this study covers. You can use a website like *www.biblegateway.com* to copy the text of a passage and print out a double-spaced copy to be able to mark on easily

A journal to write notes or prayers

Pens, colored pencils, and highlighters

A dictionary to look up unfamiliar words

HOW TO USE THIS STUDY

Begin your study time in prayer. Ask God to reveal Himself to you,
to help you understand what you are reading, and to transform you
with His Word (Psalm 119:18).

Before you read what is written in each day of the study itself, read
the assigned passages of Scripture for that day. Use your double-spaced
copy to circle, underline, highlight, draw arrows, and mark in any way
you would like to help you dig deeper as you work through a passage.

Read the daily written content provided for the current study day.

Answer the questions that appear at the end of each study day.

HOW TO STUDY THE BIBLE

The inductive method provides tools for deeper and more intentional Bible study.
To study the Bible inductively, work through the steps below after
reading background information on the book.

1 OBSERVATION & COMPREHENSION
Key question: What does the text say?

After reading the daily Scripture in its entirety at least once, begin working
with smaller portions of the Scripture. Read a passage of Scripture repetitively,
and then mark the following items in the text:

- Key or repeated words and ideas
- Key themes
- Transition words (Ex: therefore, but, because, if/then, likewise, etc.)
- Lists
- Comparisons & Contrasts
- Commands
- Unfamiliar words (look these up in a dictionary)
- Questions you have about the text

2 INTERPRETATION
Key question: What does the text mean?

Once you have annotated the text, work through the following steps to
help you interpret its meaning:

- Read the passage in other versions for a better understanding of the text.
- Read cross-references to help interpret Scripture with Scripture.
- Paraphrase or summarize the passage to check for understanding.
- Identify how the text reflects the metanarrative of Scripture, which is the story of creation, fall, redemption, and restoration.
- Read trustworthy commentaries if you need further insight into the meaning of the passage.

3 APPLICATION
Key Question: How should the truth of this passage change me?

Bible study is not merely an intellectual pursuit. The truths about God, ourselves, and the gospel that we discover in Scripture should produce transformation in our hearts and lives. Answer the following questions as you consider what you have learned in your study:

- What attributes of God's character are revealed in the passage?

  Consider places where the text directly states the character of God, as well as how His character is revealed through His words and actions.

- What do I learn about myself in light of who God is?

  Consider how you fall short of God's character, how the text reveals your sin nature, and what it says about your new identity in Christ.

- How should this truth change me?

  A passage of Scripture may contain direct commands telling us what to do or warnings about sins to avoid in order to help us grow in holiness. Other times our application flows out of seeing ourselves in light of God's character. As we pray and reflect on how God is calling us to change in light of His Word, we should be asking questions like, "How should I pray for God to change my heart?" and "What practical steps can I take toward cultivating habits of holiness?"

THE ATTRIBUTES OF GOD

ETERNAL

God has no beginning and no end. He always was, always is, and always will be.

HAB. 1:12 / REV. 1:8 / IS. 41:4

FAITHFUL

God is incapable of anything but fidelity. He is loyally devoted to His plan and purpose.

2 TIM. 2:13 / DEUT. 7:9
HEB. 10:23

GOOD

God is pure; there is no defilement in Him. He is unable to sin, and all He does is good.

GEN. 1:31 / PS. 34:8 / PS. 107:1

GRACIOUS

God is kind, giving us gifts and benefits we do not deserve.

2 KINGS 13:23 / PS. 145:8
IS. 30:18

HOLY

God is undefiled and unable to be in the presence of defilement. He is sacred and set-apart.

REV. 4:8 / LEV. 19:2 / HAB. 1:13

INCOMPREHENSIBLE & TRANSCENDENT

God is high above and beyond human understanding. He is unable to be fully known.

PS. 145:3 / IS. 55:8-9
ROM. 11:33-36

IMMUTABLE

God does not change. He is the same yesterday, today, and tomorrow.

1 SAM. 15:29 / ROM. 11:29
JAMES 1:17

INFINITE

God is limitless. He exhibits all of His attributes perfectly and boundlessly.

ROM. 11:33-36 / IS. 40:28
PS. 147:5

JEALOUS

God is desirous of receiving the praise and affection He rightly deserves.

EX. 20:5 / DEUT. 4:23-24
JOSH. 24:19

JUST

God governs in perfect justice. He acts in accordance with justice. In Him, there is no wrongdoing or dishonesty.

IS. 61:8 / DEUT. 32:4 / PS. 146:7-9

LOVING

God is eternally, enduringly, steadfastly loving and affectionate. He does not forsake or betray His covenant love.

JN. 3:16 / EPH. 2:4-5 / 1 JN. 4:16

MERCIFUL

God is compassionate,
withholding from us the
wrath that we deserve.

TITUS 3:5 / PS. 25:10
LAM. 3:22-23

OMNIPOTENT

God is all-powerful;
His strength is unlimited.

MAT. 19:26 / JOB 42:1-2
JER. 32:27

OMNIPRESENT

God is everywhere;
His presence is near
and permeating.

PROV. 15:3 / PS. 139:7-10
JER. 23:23-24

OMNISCIENT

God is all-knowing;
there is nothing
unknown to Him.

PS. 147:4 / I JN. 3:20
HEB. 4:13

PATIENT

God is long-suffering and
enduring. He gives ample
opportunity for people
to turn toward Him.

ROM. 2:4 / 2 PET. 3:9 / PS. 86:15

SELF-EXISTENT

God was not created
but exists by His
power alone.

PS. 90:1-2 / JN. 1:4 / JN. 5:26

SELF-SUFFICIENT

God has no needs and
depends on nothing, but
everything depends on God.

IS. 40:28-31 / ACTS 17:24-25
PHIL. 4:19

SOVEREIGN

God governs over all things;
He is in complete control.

COL. 1:17 / PS. 24:1-2
1 CHRON. 29:11-12

TRUTHFUL

God is our measurement
of what is fact. By Him
are we able to discern
true and false.

JN. 3:33 / ROM. 1:25 / JN. 14:6

WISE

God is infinitely
knowledgeable and is
judicious with His
knowledge.

IS. 46:9-10 / IS. 55:9 / PROV. 3:19

WRATHFUL

God stands in opposition to
all that is evil. He enacts
judgment according to
His holiness, righteousness,
and justice.

PS. 69:24 / JN. 3:36 / ROM. 1:18

Creation

In the beginning, God created the universe. He made the world and everything in it. He created humans in His own image to be His representatives on the earth.

Fall

The first humans, Adam and Eve, disobeyed God by eating from the fruit of the Tree of Knowledge of Good and Evil. Their disobedience impacted the whole world. The punishment for sin is death, and because of Adam's original sin, all humans are sinful and condemned to death.

Redemption

God sent His Son to become a human and redeem His people. Jesus Christ lived a sinless life but died on the cross to pay the penalty for sin. He resurrected from the dead and ascended into heaven. All who put their faith in Jesus are saved from death and freely receive the gift of eternal life.

Restoration

One day, Jesus Christ will return again and restore all that sin destroyed. He will usher in a new heaven and new earth where all who trust in Him will live eternally with glorified bodies in the presence of God.

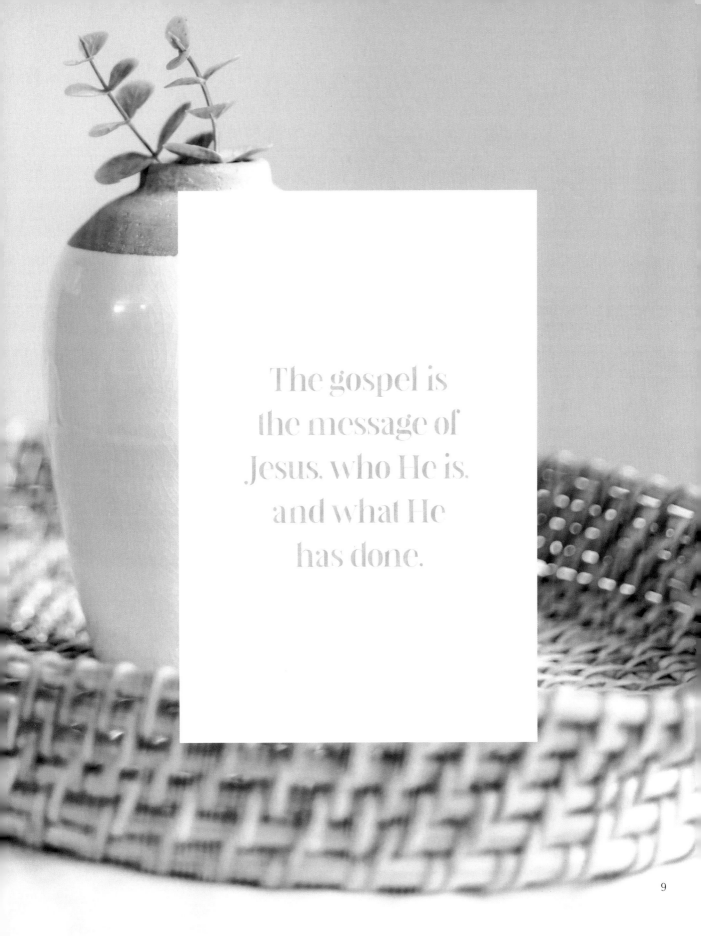

The gospel is
the message of
Jesus, who He is,
and what He
has done.

In This Study

A Prayer to Begin

Lord, as we begin this new study,
may You be glorified and Your name lifted high.
Burden our hearts for the lost.
Open our eyes to the needy.
Equip us, and give us courage.
May our lives reflect Your purity and love.
Help us understand our calling and
the joy of our salvation.
Make us faithful ambassadors of Your name,
and help us obey You, no matter the cost.

Evangelistic Conversations Log

DATE: _____ NAME: _____

PART OF THE GOSPEL SHARED: ☐ *God* ☐ *Sin* ☐ *Jesus* ☐ *Response*

REFLECTIONS FROM THE CONVERSATION: _____

_____

FOLLOW-UP: _____

_____

DATE: _____ NAME: _____

PART OF THE GOSPEL SHARED: ☐ *God* ☐ *Sin* ☐ *Jesus* ☐ *Response*

REFLECTIONS FROM THE CONVERSATION: _____

_____

FOLLOW-UP: _____

_____

DATE: _____ NAME: _____

PART OF THE GOSPEL SHARED: ☐ *God* ☐ *Sin* ☐ *Jesus* ☐ *Response*

REFLECTIONS FROM THE CONVERSATION: _____

_____

FOLLOW-UP: _____

_____

DATE: _____ NAME: _____

PART OF THE GOSPEL SHARED: ☐ *God* ☐ *Sin* ☐ *Jesus* ☐ *Response*

REFLECTIONS FROM THE CONVERSATION: _____

_____

FOLLOW-UP: _____

_____

DATE: _____ NAME: _____

PART OF THE GOSPEL SHARED: ☐ *God*   ☐ *Sin*   ☐ *Jesus*   ☐ *Response*

REFLECTIONS FROM THE CONVERSATION: _____

_____

FOLLOW-UP: _____

_____

DATE: _____ NAME: _____

PART OF THE GOSPEL SHARED: ☐ *God*   ☐ *Sin*   ☐ *Jesus*   ☐ *Response*

REFLECTIONS FROM THE CONVERSATION: _____

_____

FOLLOW-UP: _____

_____

DATE: _____ NAME: _____

PART OF THE GOSPEL SHARED: ☐ *God*   ☐ *Sin*   ☐ *Jesus*   ☐ *Response*

REFLECTIONS FROM THE CONVERSATION: _____

_____

FOLLOW-UP: _____

_____

DATE: _____ NAME: _____

PART OF THE GOSPEL SHARED: ☐ *God*   ☐ *Sin*   ☐ *Jesus*   ☐ *Response*

REFLECTIONS FROM THE CONVERSATION: _____

_____

FOLLOW-UP: _____

_____

"To share the gospel, we must know what it is."

What is the Gospel?

|

READ GENESIS 1:1, GENESIS 3:1-21,
1 CORINTHIANS 15:3-4, AND REVELATION 21:1-4

"God was the first ever missionary when in Genesis 3:8
he went out in search of two sinners who had rebelled against
Him in order to bring them back into fellowship with Him."

EDDY HO

When you hear the word "evangelism," what comes to mind? Do you think of a pastor preaching to the lost or serving meals at the homeless shelter? Do you picture a person handing out tracts to strangers on the street or having intimate conversations over dinner? For years, the word "evangelism" has been twisted and confused because of modern-day misadventures. Although the word itself is biblical and even commanded in Scripture, many instinctually recoil upon hearing it because of unpleasant experiences.

The word "evangelism" can also bring great anxiety. Maybe you picked up this study with a nervous desire to share your faith, but you do not know how. Or maybe you have never heard of evangelism and have no idea what it is or where to start. Over the next few weeks, we will be studying the theology of evangelism. In other words, we will study why and how should we share the gospel? We will also address common fears or concerns around evangelism, as well as effective strategies for sharing the gospel. But first, we must lay a foundation for sharing our faith. To share the gospel, we must know what it is. While our methods of sharing the gospel may change, the gospel itself is unchanging in its substance.

So what is the gospel? The gospel is the message of Jesus—who He is and what He has done. While there are many ways to share the good news of salvation offered to those who believe in Jesus, the content of the gospel remains the same: Jesus, who is fully God and fully man, died for our sins and rose again, defeating His enemy so that there is now no condemnation for those who believe, but rather eternal life with Him.

Another way to tell this story is through the categories of creation, fall, redemption, and restoration. This framework presents the gospel story in context from start to finish, from Genesis to Revelation.

CREATION
God
——————————

In the beginning, God created everything. He made the trees, plants, and animals, and everything was good. In Genesis 1-3, we learn a lot about who God is and what He requires:

- *He is the Creator who made and designed a good world. When God created the world, there was no sickness, pain, or death. Everything was good and as it should be.*

- *He is our Maker, first giving life to Adam and Even who lived in perfect intimacy with Him. He gives breath to every living thing and holds all things together.*

- *God requires obedience to His commands, giving Adam and Eve one prohibition: do not eat from the tree of the knowledge of good and evil.*

- *He is not far off but comes near to His people and communicates with them.*

- *God knows all and has authority over everyone and everything.*

SCRIPTURE FOR FURTHER STUDY:
GENESIS 1, EXODUS 34:6-7, PSALM 19

FALL
Sin
——————————

In Genesis 3, Adam and Eve were tempted to disbelieve God and chose to break God's rule. By eating the fruit, sin was introduced into humanity, and Adam and Eve's perfect intimacy with God was broken. They were cast out of the garden of Eden, and death was brought into the world. Their sin separated them from God, affecting every area of life. Though the term "sin" may feel out-dated to some, we can all recognize its effects today—corruption, genocide, adultery, addiction, and broken relationships. Although

God is perfectly loving, He is also perfectly just and cannot tolerate sin (Habakkuk 1:13). Because of the fall, we are all born into sin, which separates us from God.

SCRIPTURE FOR FURTHER STUDY: GENESIS 3, EPHESIANS 2:1-5, ROMANS 3:19, 23

REDEMPTION
Christil

The sin of Adam and Eve did not take God by surprise. God planned a path of redemption for His people from the beginning and orchestrated a way for us to be saved. In Genesis 3:15, God promised that He would send someone who would crush the head of the serpent (Satan) and who would be crushed for us. God came near to His people, making a way for them to be right with Him by sending His Son. Jesus lived the perfect life that we could never live and died the death that we deserve. On the cross, He paid for our sins, destroying the power of sin and death. And three days later, He rose from the grave. Whoever believes in Him will no longer be condemned in their sin but be forgiven and called a child of God.

SCRIPTURE FOR FURTHER STUDY: GENESIS 3:15, 2 CORINTHIANS 5:21, 1 PETER 2:24

RESTORATION
Response

One day, God will return to make all things new. For those who believe in Him, there will be no more pain or sickness as we are united again with Jesus. We will finally be set free from the lingering brokenness in the world and experience perfect intimacy with the Father. But for those who do not repent of their sins and submit to God, there will be judgment and eternal condemnation. God does not delight in any person's condemnation and freely offers the gift of salvation to all who would receive it.

SCRIPTURE FOR FURTHER STUDY: 2 PETER 3:9, MATTHEW 13:37-43, REVELATION 21:1-4

The entire Bible points to this simple story and answers the age-old questions: Who made us? What's wrong with me? What's the solution, and how can I be saved? Thankfully, God has not left us alone. He has left us His Spirit that dwells within believers to equip and prepare us for the work of the Lord. He has also given us the Bible, providing everything that we need to know about life and godliness through His Word.

Have you ever yielded yourself to Jesus by repenting of your sins and trusting in Him? If so, describe your conversion experience below. If not, what are your reservations about doing this?

_____

_____

_____

_____

_____

Read Genesis 1, Genesis 3:15, and 2 Peter 3:9, and write out a two-minute gospel presentation using creation, fall, redemption, and restoration.

_____

_____

_____

_____

_____

_____

_____

_____

_____

_____

_____

_____

Read through your gospel presentation several times out loud. Record yourself speaking the message of the gospel, and repeat this process until it feels natural. The more often we repeat the gospel, the more comfortable we will become sharing it with others.

Bonus: Find a friend, and practice sharing the gospel with each other.

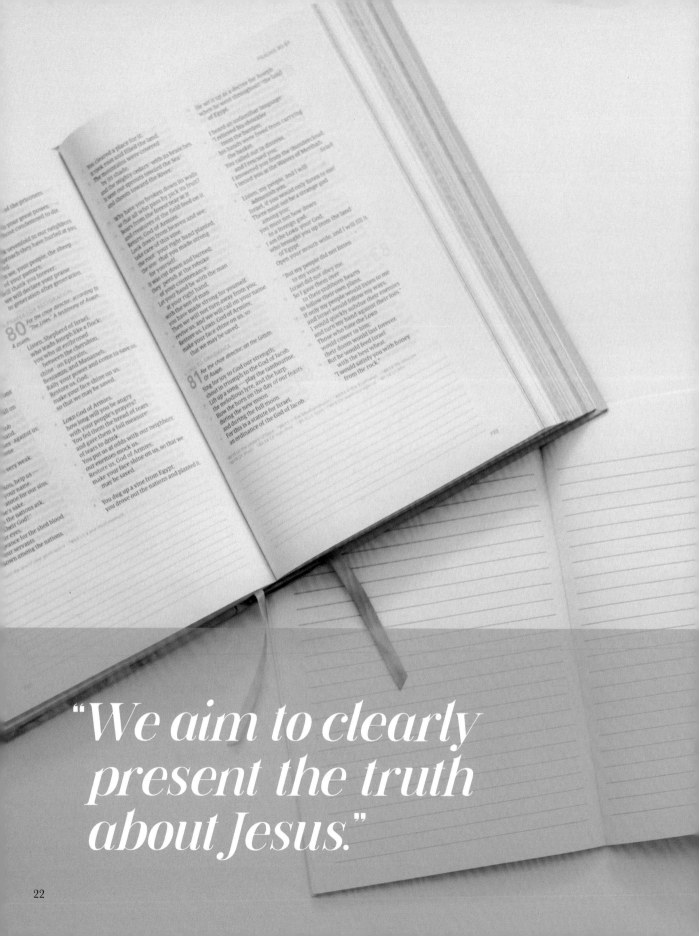

"We aim to clearly present the truth about Jesus."

What is Evangelism?

|

READ MATTHEW 28:18-20, JOHN 3:16-17, JOHN 20:21

"To evangelize…does not mean to win converts…but simply to announce the good news, irrespective of the results."

JOHN STOTT

The word "evangelism" is used throughout Scripture and is directly modeled in the life of Jesus and the disciples' lives. In the Old Testament, the Hebrew word for "evangelism" was *besorah* (noun) or *basar* (verb) meaning "glad tidings" or "to announce (glad news)." It often connoted a positive victory of public significance, such as a victory in battle or the ascension of a king.

Look up Isaiah 40:9, Isaiah 52:7, and 2 Samuel 18:26-27. What do you learn about the word *basar* or "good news" in these contexts?

_____

_____

_____

In the New Testament, the Greek word for "evangelism" is *euangelion* (noun) or *euangelizō* (verb), referring to the story of Jesus. It was used 76 times in the New Testament, 60 of these by Paul alone. The ancient Greek interpretation for this word is "to announce good news, especially the gospel." The message of God's redemptive work is indeed good news for all who believe!

As He ascended into heaven, Jesus commanded His followers, "Go, therefore, and make disciples of all nations, baptizing them in the name of the Father and of the Son and of the Holy Spirit, teaching them to observe everything I have commanded you. And remember, I am with you always, to the end of the age" (Matthew 28:19-20). His parting words give us insight into the grand mission we now have as His followers. Every believer is now called to go and make disciples by teaching others the truths found in Scripture. Doing so first starts with evangelism, or sharing the message of the gospel, and continues by discipling believers in the Word.

Because evangelism is sharing the good news of Jesus, gospel clarity is of utmost importance. As Paul shared the gospel, he sought to persuade those listening to believe its simple message. Recognizing its eternal value, Paul made his sole aim in life to preach the gospel, even when it cost him his life. He rejoiced when others preached the gospel, even with poor motives, because he knew that the gospel alone has the power to save (Philippians 1:15-20). Even as Paul shared the gospel, he wanted to make sure that his message was clear:

> Now I want to make clear for you, brothers and sisters, the gospel I preached to you, which you received, on which you have taken your stand and by which you are being saved, if you hold to the message I preached to you—unless you believed in vain. For I passed on to you as most important what I also received: that Christ died for our sins according to the Scriptures, that he was buried, that he was raised on the third day according to the Scriptures, and that he appeared to Cephas, then to the Twelve. Then he appeared to over five hundred brothers and sisters at one time; most of them are still alive, but some have fallen asleep (1 Corinthians 15:1-6).

What are the key parts of the gospel as described by Paul?

_____

_____

_____

_____

_____

_____

_____

_____

_____

_____

"Because evangelism is sharing the good news of Jesus. gospel clarity is of utmost importance."

It is essential to understand that evangelism is of primary importance to all believers. While there are many ways to share the gospel, it is also important to note what sharing the gospel is not. The gospel is not:

- *Passing out meals at the homeless shelter. While serving the poor and homeless is an important command in Scripture, in order to share the gospel, we must also use words.*

- *Primarily a story about how to get to heaven. While the gospel does offer saving power to those who believe, it is primarily about what God has done, not how to get a better life. In the same way, the gospel is not a message about having your best life on Earth. Those who follow Jesus follow a Savior who was crucified and whose followers were killed for their faith. When we promise a trial-free life to those who believe in Jesus, we preach a false gospel.*

- *Simply the message that God loves us. While sharing the message that God loves us is true, it is only a part of the gospel hope for our lives. If it does not include the message of God, sin, Jesus, or repentance. It is not the full gospel.*

- *Telling people that their sin is bad without offering the hope found in Christ. While it is true that sin—from lying to murder—is abhorrent to a holy God, this narrative does not tell of Jesus's payment for sins on the cross or the hope offered through belief in Him.*

- *A personal testimony—the story of God's work in our lives can be a great tool to use in evangelism, but it itself is not the gospel. We need to invite others to believe the message about Jesus's life, death, and resurrection to find eternal life themselves.*

In his book, *Evangelism: How the Whole Church Speaks of Jesus*, J. Mack Stiles defines evangelism as sharing the good news of the gospel with the goal of persuading others. When we share the gospel, we aim to clearly present the truth about Jesus, who was fully God and fully man and came to save sinners through His perfect life, death, and resurrection. Jesus is our perfect teacher, and His mission was clear. He desired for all to be saved and gave His life as a ransom for many. He invested in a select few men who God would use to spread the gospel throughout the world.

As we share the gospel, we must maintain gospel clarity and remember that God is with us. We can do nothing on our own, but by relying on God's power through prayer and in faithfully proclaiming the gospel to the lost, we will see Him do great things. The work of evangelism can be slow-going. Many people must hear the message of the gospel multiple times before believing. It demands wisdom to know when to share and with whom. Most importantly, it requires the work of the Spirit to open blind eyes and bring eternal life.

What are your initial feelings when you hear the word "evangelism"? Why?

What is your motive for picking up this study, and what are your goals for the next six weeks? Sample goals may include growing in boldness, clarity of the gospel, or gospel sharing techniques.

Consider Matthew 28:18-20. What is the call of every believer?

Recount successful and unsuccessful methods of sharing your faith.

Brainstorming Relationships

Some people think that evangelism means going up to strangers and sharing the gospel. While it is not less than that, it is much more. The primary way we see evangelism carried out by the local church is within preexisting relationships—through the network of family, friends, and acquaintances that God has already placed around us. God has put us in this specific place and time in history, surrounded by a network of believing and unbelieving friends to glorify Him and share the gospel with those around us.

Spend a few minutes brainstorming the non-Christians who God has put in your life. Create a list of family, friends, co-workers, and neighbors who do not know the Lord:

FAMILY
(INCLUDING EXTENDED FAMILY)

FRIENDS

NEIGHBORS

_____
_____
_____
_____
_____
_____
_____
_____
_____
_____
_____
_____
_____
_____
_____
_____

CO-WORKERS
AND ACQUAINTANCES

_____
_____
_____
_____
_____
_____
_____
_____
_____
_____
_____
_____
_____
_____
_____
_____

Spend time praying over these friends and family. If you completed this exercise with only a few names written down, brainstorm ways to engage with unbelievers throughout the day. Use this as an encouragement to pursue hobbies or relationships with non-believers. Become a regular at your local coffee shop, or go to the gym at the same time each day. Better still, talk to a friend from church and join a club, or start a hobby together to expand your network of non-believers. Get to know your co-workers' and neighbors' names, and pray for opportunities to meet those who do not know the Lord.

"One of the primary ways God moves through His people is through prayer."

Importance of Prayer in Evangelism

READ MATTHEW 9:37-38, MATTHEW 17:20-21,
PHILIPPIANS 4:6-7

"I have felt the impact of your prayer in these past weeks. I am
certain now that nothing has had a more powerful influence
on this life of mine than your prayers."

JIM ELLIOT

The original Christian evangelists were men and women who walked with Jesus: His disciples. Jesus did not pick the smartest, most religious men of His day to be heralds of this message. Instead, He chose ordinary, humble men. Why did He focus on a select few when there were so many others who were more qualified? Surely there were more equipped and religious men who would have fit the bill to become the first leaders of His church. Instead, God chose "uneducated and ordinary men" in order to show His abounding and sufficient power (Acts 4:13). Not many were wise or highly esteemed so that God alone would get the glory. This should fill us with great hope. God can use us too!

One of the primary ways God moves through His people is through prayer. As A.T. Pierson said, "There has never been a spiritual awakening in any country or locality that did not begin in united prayer." Prayer preceded every revival in religious history, including the Protestant Reformation and the Great Awakenings of the 18th and 19th centuries. God alone has the power to save, and through prayer, God mysteriously moves to accomplish His salvific and redemptive purposes.

As we pray, God works not only in the lives of our lost friends and family but also within our hearts. God gives us a burden for the lost, helping us to see opportunities to share the gospel. He gives us boldness and words beyond our natural personalities or abilities. He floods our hearts with a supernatural love for those around us. In John 6:63, Jesus says, "The Spirit is the one who gives life. The flesh doesn't help at all. The words that I have spoken to you are spirit and are life." While we are called to share the gospel faithfully, we cannot change hearts. Only God has the power to bring souls from death to life, opening the eyes of the lost to their sin and leading them to repentance. How then should we pray?

1. Pray for God's glory on Earth.

Pause now to praise God for who He is. Ask the Lord to reveal His glory to the world, bringing many sons and daughters to know Him. Pray that your local church would honor God and be a light to your city. Write out your prayers below.

_____

_____

_____

_____

_____

2. Pray for personal revival.

We are to live holy and loving lives that reflect our Savior. When we are living in open rebellion to God's commands, those around us will notice. If we are anxious about death or the political climate like our neighbors, we are not reflecting the eternal joy we have in Christ that is not dependent on any earthly circumstance.

Pray now for personal revival and conviction, especially as it relates to evangelism. Pray that the Lord would reveal areas of hidden sin in your life and that you would remain pure in the world. Pray for boldness and opportunities to share the gospel and for the words to present the message of Jesus clearly. Pray for a love for those around you who do not believe in the gospel.

_____

_____

_____

_____

_____

3. Pray for the lost.

In Romans 10:1, Paul says it is his "heart's desire and prayer to God" that the Israelites be saved. He prayed fervently, willing even to give up his own salvation if it meant that they could be saved. He passionately prayed for boldness to share the gospel with the lost and for opportunities to do so (Colossians 4:3-4).

Spend time praying for your lost friends and family. Pray that God would open their hearts, convict them of sin, and help them see Jesus's redemptive love. Pray that God would give them a saving knowledge of the truth and repentance that leads to salvation. With Paul, pray that "Perhaps God will grant them repentance leading them to the knowledge of the truth. Then they may come to their senses and escape the trap of the devil, who has taken them captive to do his will" (2 Timothy 2:25-26).

Pray for the whole world.

In Matthew 9:37-38, Jesus says, "The harvest is abundant, but the workers are few. Therefore, pray to the Lord of the harvest to send out workers into his harvest." We are called to pray for God to send people to share the gospel around the world.

Spend time praying that the Lord would send out missionaries to the ends of the earth to share the gospel with those who do not have access to the Bible. Pray for the poor, for the persecuted church, and for faithful men and women to know God's Word and preach it to the ends of the earth.

AS WE PRAY, GOD WORKS NOT ONLY IN THE LIVES OF OUR LOST FRIENDS AND FAMILY BUT ALSO WITHIN OUR HEARTS.

Write down any personal reflections from your time in prayer.
Bonus: Tell a friend what you have learned!

_____

_____

_____

_____

Do you regularly pray for the lost around you? How could you be more faithful in this practice?

_____

_____

_____

_____

Read 1 Corinthians 1:26-31. What does this show you about who God chooses and how He uses regular, ordinary men and women?

_____

_____

_____

_____

Read Revelation 7:9-17. How does this future vision of all nations worshiping God inspire you to action today?

_____

_____

_____

_____

"There has never been a spiritual awakening in any country or locality that did not begin in united prayer."

A.T. PIERSON

Sin and Salvation

As you are learning to share your faith, consider the words that the Bible uses to describe sin and salvation. This will be help you communicate the power of the gospel to the specific needs and desires of your lost friends, family members, or neighbors:

HOW THE BIBLE DESCRIBES OUR SIN

EXAMPLE	SCRIPTURE
Failing to keep God's law	1 John 3:4
Falling short of God's glory	Romans 3:23
Guilt	Jeremiah 3:13
Shame	Isaiah 42:17
Idolatry	Exodus 20:3-6
Self-righteousness	Romans 10:3
Pride	Romans 12:16
Worthless	Job 15:31
Not trusting God	Jeremiah 17:5
Rebellion	Isaiah 66:24
Omission of something we are supposed to do	James 4:17
Doing something evil	2 Timothy 3:2-6, Colossians 3:5-6
Unholiness	1 Timothy 1:9
Doing something with the wrong motivation	James 4:3
Disobedience	Romans 1:30, Ephesians 5:6

HOW THE BIBLE DESCRIBES OUR SALVATION

EXAMPLE	SCRIPTURE
Forgiven	1 John 1:9
Set free	Romans 8:2, John 8:31-33
Saved	Ephesians 2:8-9
Born again	1 Peter 1:23
Adopted	Romans 8:14-16
Delivered from sin	2 Corinthians 5:21
Bought at a price	1 Corinthians 6:20
Called a child of God	1 John 3:1
Under God's grace	Romans 6:14
Made holy	2 Timothy 1:9
Washed	1 Corinthians 6:11
Justified	Galatians 3:24
Made at peace with God	Romans 5:1
Redeemed	Colossians 1:14, Ephesians 1:7
Made into a new creation	2 Corinthians 5:17
Brought to an everlasting hope	Ephesians 1:18
No longer a slave to sin, but instead a slave to righteousness	Romans 6:15-23
Restored	Revelation 21:1-5
Reconciled	2 Corinthians 5:18-19

"God's ways are perfect."

Spiritual Warfare in Evangelism

READ EPHESIANS 6:10-20, 1 JOHN 5:8

"The gospel is only good news if it gets there in time."

CARL F. H. HENRY

As we evangelize, seeking to share the good news of the gospel and persuading others to believe it, we will find ourselves engaging in God's global mission. In this battle, He has promised never to leave us nor forsake us, and through the Bible, we know the end of the story. God is the winner, and will one day return to make all things right. As we prepare to share the gospel, it is important to remember that we are entering into a cosmic battle, and there are greater forces at work in the war over people's souls. Just as a soldier does not go into battle unarmed, we must first put on our spiritual armor, clothed with the protection God Himself has provided. As it is written in 2 Timothy 2:4, "No one serving as a soldier gets entangled in the concerns of civilian life; he seeks to please the commanding officer."

THE PROBLEM

Why are we in a spiritual battle? While the specifics of spiritual warfare are unclear in the Bible, we know that God's ways are perfect, and He gives us a choice to obey or disobey Him. He gave this choice to the angels as well, and Satan did not want to worship God (Isaiah 14:12-14, Ezekiel 28:14-18). In Genesis 3, when Adam and Eve fell because they listened to the serpent instead of God, mankind was also condemned. Because of this, we were all born into darkness—blind and unable to save ourselves. When Jesus came and died on the cross, He saved us from our sin and brought us from darkness to light. He rescued us when we were powerless to redeem ourselves. But for those who do not yet believe in Jesus, "the god of this age has blinded the minds of the unbelievers to keep them from seeing the light of the gospel of the glory of Christ, who is the image of God" (2 Corinthians 4:4). They are still blinded and in rebellion against a holy God. There is a real battle going on over the souls.

Satan's methods are not creative, nor are they new (John 8:44). From the garden of Eden until today, we see him promoting disunity and disobedience (Genesis 3:1-4). He wants us to doubt God or to doubt who God has made us to be in Christ. He wants us to become discouraged or proud and to create division within the church (2 Thessalonians 2:9-10, 2 Peter 2:1-4, Revelation 12:9). Indeed, how many have been turned off from the Lord because the church has hurt them? We also learn in Scripture that Satan's role never justifies or excuses human responsibility (James 4:7-8). Even though we may be tempted, we are each responsible before God for our actions and decisions (James 1:14, Ephesians 4:27, 1 John 5:18).

The battle is real, but we need not be afraid. In the book of Job, we see that Satan can do nothing without God permitting it (Job 1). For the believer, God will use every trial for their good (Romans 8:28). When we trust in Jesus, He sends His Spirit to live within us. God is stronger than Satan and promises to protect His children. While we need not fear, neither should we ignore the enemy, but rather be equipped for battle.

THE SOLUTION

The hope in battle is found in Christ. He has defeated the powers of sin and death, and He helps us withstand temptation (1 Corinthians 10:13) and resist the devil (James 4:7). He has also given us spiritual armor for battle. Read about this armor in Ephesians 6:10-20:

> Finally, be strengthened by the Lord and by his vast strength. Put on the full armor of God so that you can stand against the schemes of the devil. For our struggle is not against flesh and blood, but against the rulers, against the authorities, against the cosmic powers of this darkness, against evil, spiritual forces in the heavens. For this reason take up the full armor of God, so that you may be able to resist in the evil day, and having prepared everything, to take your stand. Stand, therefore, with truth like a belt around your waist, righteousness like armor on your chest, and your feet sandaled with readiness for the gospel of peace. In every situation take up the shield of faith with which you can extinguish all the flaming arrows of the evil one. Take the helmet of salvation and the sword of the Spirit—which is the word of God. Pray at all times in the Spirit with every prayer and request, and stay alert with all perseverance and intercession for all the saints. Pray also for me, that the message may be given to me when I open my mouth to make known with boldness the mystery of the gospel. For this I am an ambassador in chains. Pray that I might be bold enough to speak about it as I should.

List the different components of the armor of God.

How do these components equip you for evangelism?

Only one of the items listed allows for active fighting in the battle.
With what do we actively fight the enemy?

Do you know God's Word and feel equipped to use it to fight the schemes of the enemy?
If not, what can you do to grow in this area?

Notice how Paul links spiritual warfare with God's Word and sharing the gospel. He concludes his remarks on spiritual warfare in Ephesians 6 by praying for boldness to share the gospel. We are called to cling closely to Him, obeying Him and arming ourselves in the power of His Word. We need not fear any spiritual battle, nor should we be ignorant of it either. We defeat the enemy, not in our own strength but in the Lord's.

Have you ever considered spiritual warfare? How does spiritual warfare relate to the topic of evangelism?

_____

_____

_____

_____

Read how Jesus resisted temptation in Matthew 4:1-11. What can we learn about the importance of knowing God's Word as we seek to obey God?

_____

_____

_____

_____

If we are in Christ, we need not fear spiritual warfare because we have One who is more powerful than Satan. Read Romans 16:20 and Revelation 20:10. How do these verses encourage you to stand firm in the promised victory of our King?

_____

_____

_____

_____

_____

_____

He has promised
never to leave us
nor forsake us.

Manger, Cross, and Crown
Gospel Presentation

ONE WAY TO TELL THE GOSPEL STORY IS BY SHARING
THE CATEGORIES MANGER, CROSS, AND CROWN.

MANGER

Jesus, who is fully God and fully man, came to Earth and was born
and placed in a lowly manger. While on Earth, Jesus experienced
the normal human experience. He was hungry, thirsty, and tired. He
was betrayed, abused, and abandoned. He lived a perfect life and in
doing so, fulfilled the Law's demands. The manger shows us that God
understands our struggles, and He is present with us.

CROSS

Though completely perfect, Jesus died on a cross, and in doing so,
paid the penalty for our sins. This shows us that God made a way
to pardon our sins. God is able and willing to forgive us
through the blood of Jesus.

CROWN

Jesus rose from the dead and now wears an eternal crown in victory. He is King over all and has power over everyone and everything. This shows us God's victory over the grave and the promise that He will one day return and make all things right. The crown also brings great hope in our sufferings—hope in knowing that this world is temporary, but the Kingdom of Christ endures forever.

POSSIBLE FOLLOW-UP QUESTIONS FOR THE LISTENER:

What are your thoughts about this story?

Have you ever heard this story before?

What about this story is difficult to believe?

Have you ever repented?

"It is normal to experience fear while sharing the gospel."

Common Fears Around Evangelism

READ PROVERBS 29:25, LUKE 10:2, HEBREWS 13:6

"If a commission by an earthly king is considered an honor, how can a commission by a Heavenly King be considered a sacrifice?"

DAVID LIVINGSTONE

Perhaps as you have been reading, you have noticed tension developing within your body every time the word "evangelism" is used. The thought of sharing the gospel with your friends makes you all but break out in hives. You have started to create objections in your mind like "evangelism is just not my gift" or "my friends would not be interested in spiritual things."

It is normal to experience fear while sharing the gospel. The Apostle Paul himself asked for prayers to share the gospel with boldness (Ephesians 6:20). If an apostle needed prayers for boldness, so do we. Yet while it is normal to experience anxiety in sharing the gospel, this should not be an excuse to avoid obedience. Rather than ignoring these objections or fears, we can face them directly, knowing that God's Word provides great encouragement and help to those who are afraid.

What are the primary emotions you encounter as you consider sharing your faith (excitement, terror, fear, concern, joy)?

_____

_____

_____

Write out your top objections or fears in sharing your faith.

_____

_____

_____

_____

HERE ARE A FEW COMMON OBJECTIONS AND FEARS THAT BELIEVERS FACE IN EVANGELISM:

I do not know what to say. You have come to the right place. This evangelism handbook will equip you with the essentials to share your faith. You may be afraid you will be awkward or that they will ask a question you do not know the answer to. That is okay; you do not need to know the answer to every question. "I do not know, but I will get back to you" is a perfectly acceptable response to a difficult question. It is also a response that shows humility and sincerity.

Evangelism is not my gift, or it is not my place to share with them. Evangelism is the call of every believer. In Matthew 28, Jesus gave the command for His disciples to "go and make disciples of all nations." This call applies to all believers regardless of age, country, or marital status. God has put you at a unique point in history around specific people so that you will be a light in the darkness. You have access to relationships that your pastors and other seminary grads will never have. You are called to make disciples and teach what God has commanded, both to the believer and unbeliever.

I have tried that before, but it did not turn out well. Often bad experiences in the past can hinder us from wanting to share our faith in the future. Even if we have had an awkward interaction in the past, God's mercies are new every morning, and He is with us wherever we go. Through Christ, we can run the race with perseverance and try again in

faith (Hebrews 12:1-2, Proverbs 24:16).

What if they are not interested? Sometimes we can assume that those around us would not be interested in spiritual things. We forget that every person has a deep longing for acceptance and belonging. Every person experiences the crushing weight of shame and guilt, and we live in a world where debilitating depression, shame, loneliness, and anxiety are part of the human experience. The loved ones around us need the gospel.

I am afraid of what they will think of me or how they will respond. Fear of what people think of us is called the fear of man. No one wants to look like a fool in front of others, and we can be afraid of being judged by our friends and family. We are concerned with looking good in front of others, or at least not sticking out and being the strange one. The Bible directly addresses this fear:

- *The fear of mankind is a snare, but the one who trusts in the Lord is protected (Proverbs 29:25).*

- *The Lord is my helper; I will not be afraid. What can man do to me? (Hebrews 13:6)*

We must fear God more than man and obey Him no matter what others may think of us.

I do not know any unbelievers. Perhaps based on our circumstances, we find ourselves in a Christian bubble. Perhaps we work in a Christian workplace or are at home. Maybe all of our friends and family are Christians. This realization is a great opportunity to make a change and to brainstorm fresh ways to engage with unbelievers. Perhaps you can start a new hobby with one of your Christian friends, committing to intentionally seek spiritual conversations with non-Christians who are interested in the hobby over time. Maybe you can become a regular at a local restaurant and get to know your waitress's name and story. Maybe you can invite a neighbor over for dessert one night.

Maybe you relate to one of these objections, or perhaps you have lingering concerns. Perhaps you are "too busy" or you forget that the people around you are eternal souls. Maybe you have never shared the gospel before and would like to see it modeled. At the end of the day, we must each decide whether we will follow our feelings or obey the Lord. If we understand the eternal nature of those around us and the hope found in the gospel, it should spur us on to share with others!

Paul says that he had "great sorrow and unceasing anguish in [his] heart" for Jews who did not know Christ (Romans 9:2-3). His burden for them is so great that he even wishes that they could be saved instead of him. The questions we must each answer within our hearts are: "Is the gospel really true? Is it good news? Do we love those with whom we are talking?" If we truly believe that the gospel is the only way to be saved, how could we not share it with others?

daily QUESTIONS

What are your biggest fears in sharing the gospel?

_____

_____

_____

What does the Bible have to say about these fears?

_____

_____

_____

_____

Read Paul's prayers for boldness and clarity in sharing the gospel in Ephesians 6:20 and Colossians 4:3-4. How does it encourage you that the great church planter himself asked for prayers to evangelize?

_____

_____

_____

Jesus came near and said to them.
"All authority has been given to
me in heaven and on earth.
Go, therefore, and make disciples
of all nations, baptizing them in
the name of the Father and of
the Son and of the Holy Spirit,
teaching them to observe
everything I have commanded
you. And remember: I am with
you always, to the end of the age."

MATTHEW 28:18-20

weekly REFLECTION

Review all Scripture passages from the week.

Summarize the main points from this week's Scripture readings.

What did you observe from this week's passages about God and His character?

What do this week's passages reveal about the condition of mankind and yourself?

How do these passages point to the gospel?

How should you respond to these Scriptures? What specific action steps
can you take this week to apply them in your life?

Write a prayer in response to your study of God's Word. Adore God for who He is,
confess sins He revealed in your own life, ask Him to empower you to walk in obedience,
and pray for anyone who comes to mind as you study.

"We are compelled to share the gospel with urgency, love, and compassion."

Why Share the Gospel?

READ ACTS 1:8, ROMANS 1:16, ROMANS 10:13-14,
REVELATION 7:9-10

"We have all eternity to tell of the victories won for Christ, but we have only a few hours before sunset to win them."

AMY CARMICHAEL

We have discussed what the gospel is, but why should we share it? As we begin this week's study, spend some time reflecting on why you want to share your faith and what motivates you to grow in this discipline.

_____

_____

_____

The purpose of our lives is to glorify God and enjoy Him forever (Westminster Shorter Catechism). As we seek to glorify God, faith is expressed in many ways in our lives—through worship, reading the Bible, communing with Him in prayer, and fellowship with other believers. We also demonstrate our faith by sharing the gospel with others. These acts of obedience are not done to win God's favor because if we are in Christ, we already have God's unshakable love and complete acceptance through Jesus. Instead, we share the gospel in response to God's love as an expression of worship and out of love for others.

First, we share the gospel as an act of worship to God. He is worthy of worship from every man, woman, and child, and as we share the gospel, we seek to make Him known to the ends of the earth. Although now we live by faith, one day we will see God face to face and worship Him with people from every tongue, tribe, and nation (Revelation 7:9-10). What a glorious day that will be!

Jesus's entire life was one of worship as He lived in submission to the Father's will. He made "fishers of men" out of ordinary fishermen, choosing "unlearned and ignorant" disciples who were proud, ignorant, easily offended, and rude (Acts 4:13). He devoted Himself to the few—loving them, teaching them, and training them to share the gospel. Jesus did not choose the most qualified or religious men, but those He called, He equipped to become messengers of the gospel. He spoke about His mission and invited them to join Him, saying, "The harvest is abundant, but the workers are few. Therefore, pray to the Lord of the harvest to send out workers into his harvest" (Matthew 9:37-38). Our mission is the same.

We also share the gospel out of love for others. As believers, we have tasted and seen the goodness of the Lord and found that true contentment is found only in Him. He has changed our lives abundantly, and we know that there is great joy freely available to all who come to Christ. Often we can be quick to share the things we love with others, promoting our favorite restaurants, beauty products, and vacation spots. But if we truly love those around us and want what is best for them, how could we not share about God with them? He is the source of all joy, beauty, purpose, and love. As we share the gospel, we remember that there is actually no mortal being. Every one of us will live forever, either enjoying Christ or eternally separated from Him (Matthew 25:46). Because of this, we are compelled to share the gospel with urgency, love, and compassion.

Evangelism is not to be something extraordinary or special but a normative part of the Christian life. We need not be "gifted evangelists" to share about what is important in our lives and about the One who saved us. We do not share the gospel out of selfish ambition or to win an argument. And though we aim to present Christ clearly, the wisdom of God is foolishness to the world, and we often will be rejected for it (1 Corinthians 2:14). Yet we persevere for the glory of God and out of love for our neighbor. We share the gospel because He has called us, and He is worthy.

When we encounter Christ's love, it changes us. As Paul says, "For the love of Christ compels us, since we have reached this conclusion: If one died for all, then all died…Therefore, we are ambassadors for Christ, since God is making His appeal through us. We plead on Christ's behalf, 'Be reconciled to God.'" (2 Corinthians 5:14, 20). We are compelled, pushed, and driven to share the gospel with others because of the love that we have experienced firsthand. If we find ourselves struggling with a desire to share the gospel, we must refocus our gaze on Christ, the one who has rescued us from eternal punishment and brought us into everlasting life with Him. For a while, we may assume that someone else will share the gospel with our friends and family. However, is it possible that God has placed you as an intercessor to pray for and share the gospel with your friends, family, and neighbors?

List out several characteristics of God's character that lead you to worship Him.
Spend time in prayer, worshiping Him for who He is.

_____

_____

_____

We share the gospel, not to win God's favor but because we already have it in Christ. How does this
free you from unhealthy or fear-based evangelism?

_____

_____

Read Revelation 5:6-12 and Revelation 7:9-10. How does the end of the story of the Bible propel
you to action today?

_____

_____

Write out a prayer to God confessing any fears or unbelief that you have in sharing the gospel.
Ask Him for boldness and courage to share with those around you.

_____

_____

_____

_____

_____

_____

"If we truly love those around us and want what is best for them, how could we not share about God with them?"

The Four Points of the Gospel

GOD

God created the world and everything in it. God, who is perfect, pure, and good, created man and woman in His own image and designed us to live in perfect peace and intimacy with Him.

———

Genesis 1:26-28

SIN

Mankind rebelled against God. Since the fall in Genesis 3, mankind became sinful by nature. Sickness, death, and brokenness were introduced into the world. Because of our sinful nature, we are cut off—separated from the one and only, perfect God.

———

Genesis 3, Romans 3:23

RESPONSE

God calls us to repent of our sins and place our faith in Jesus, trusting in His perfect life, death, and resurrection. When we turn from our sins and believe the gospel, we are reconciled to God through His Son. God also gives us His Spirit to help us, guide us, and enable us to live godly lives. He promises that one day He will come again to make all things right, and we will live eternally with Him.

———

Mark 1:15, Acts 20:21,
Romans 10:9-10, Acts 17:30, John 1:12

CHRIST

God provided a way for us to be right with Him again by sending His Son Jesus into the world. Jesus, who was fully God and fully man, lived a perfect, sinless life. He died on the cross for our sins and took on the full wrath that we deserve. In exchange, all who believe in Jesus will receive His righteousness and be at peace with God again. Jesus offered Himself up to the Father as the perfect sacrifice, fully able to pay the infinite depth that our sins owe. On the third day, He rose from the grave, declaring victory over death and sin.

———

John 1:1, 3:16-17; 1 Timothy 2:5;
Hebrews 7:26; Romans 3:21-26, 4:25;
Acts 2:24; 1 Corinthians 15:20-22,
2 Corinthians 5:21

"The hope of the gospel compels us to action."

The Four Calls of Evangelism

READ LUKE 16:19-31, ACTS 16:9, ROMANS 9:2-3

"'Not called!' did you say? 'Not heard the call,' I think you should say. Put your ear down to the Bible, and hear Him bid you go and pull sinners out of the fire of sin. Put your ear down to the burdened, agonized heart of humanity, and listen to its pitiful wail for help. Go stand by the gates of hell, and hear the damned entreat you to go to their father's house and bid their brothers and sisters and servants and masters not to come there. Then look Christ in the face—whose mercy you have professed to obey—and tell Him whether you will join heart and soul and body and circumstances in the march to publish His mercy to the world."

WILLIAM BOOTH, FOUNDER OF SALVATION ARMY

As Christians, the hope of the gospel compels us to action. We were brought from death to life by the mercy of God. We have been saved from sin, guilt, and shame. How could we not desire the same salvation for our families, friends, and neighbors? We also see the call to share the gospel clearly expressed within the Scriptures themselves. This call comes from above, below, beside, and within.

The *call to share the gospel from above* is from God Himself, who has clearly commanded us throughout the Bible to proclaim who He is. One of the last things Jesus instructed the disciples to do before He ascended into heaven was to go and "make disciples of all nations, baptizing them" and teaching them about God (Matthew 28:18-20). He said this again in Acts 1:8, sending the disciples to share His story in Jerusalem, Judea, Samaria, and to the ends of the earth. This same call applies to us today. As Christians, we are to share God's Word and make disciples wherever we are—even to the ends of the earth.

The *call from below* is revealed in Luke 16:19-31 with the story of Lazarus and the rich man. In this story, we are introduced to an unnamed rich man, who had lived extravagantly on earth, eating and drinking with royalty. Outside his gate was poor Lazarus who longed to eat even the crumbs from the rich man's table and who was sick and hungry, with sores all over his body. When both men died, the poor man went to heaven while the rich man, who had not trusted in God for his salvation, went to hell.

From hell, the rich man looked up in misery and saw Abraham with Lazarus in heaven. He cried out, "Father...I beg you to send [Lazarus] to my father's house—because I have five brothers—to warn them, so they won't also come to this place of torment" (Luke 16:27-28). Abraham responded that his family's hearts were so hard that they would not repent even if a man rose from the dead to warn them. Even still, the man called out from below, pleading for someone to go and preach the gospel to his living family members. From this story, we see the urgency of sharing the gospel with others while they are still alive. God calls us to share the gospel with our friends and family while they have the opportunity to respond.

We see the *call from beside* in Acts 16:9 when Paul had a vision of a man from Macedonia asking him to go and tell him how to be saved. Later in Acts 16:30, God also compelled a jailer to ask Paul directly how they can be saved. Many of our friends are inwardly longing for relief from guilt, shame, and hopelessness. There are hungry people all over the world, and we have been given the bread of life. How could we not share it with them?

Finally, we have a *call from within*, which is born in our relationship with Jesus. In Romans 9:2-3, Paul expresses a burning desire to be used by God to tell others the good news. We see this in the lives of men and women throughout Scripture, such as Peter, James, and even Isaiah, when he says, "Here am I, send me" (Isaiah 6:8). As Christians, the love of Christ compels us to go to others and plead with them to be reconciled to God (Romans 5:14-15, 20). We have tasted the goodness of the Lord and long to share Him with others.

We have the call from all directions to share the gospel because in order for someone to be saved, that person must hear the gospel and believe it. We are not saved by being born into a Christian family or because we go to church. We are not saved by being a good person or by giving money to the poor. We are saved when, recognizing that we are sinners in need of a Savior, we repent of our sins and believe in the finished work of Christ. This truth necessitates the need for us to share the gospel with others so that they too can hear about Jesus and be saved. As Paul says in Romans 10:14-15:

> How, then, can they call on him they have not believed in? And how can they believe without hearing about him? And how can they hear without a preacher? And how can they preach unless they are sent? As it is written: How beautiful are the feet of those who bring good news.

So then, we must hear the good news of the gospel to be saved. But what about those who have never heard about Jesus? In Scripture, we see that God has revealed His nature to the world through His creation (Romans 1:20) and within our hearts (Ecclesiastes 3:11). The problem is that we have rebelled against God and have chosen to worship a god of our own creation. In many countries, people worship statues, idols, or fake gods, while in the West, we often elevate material goods, status, or even our reputation. We make gods out of success, happiness, family, or travel, expecting them to provide ultimate satisfaction and purpose. We worship them, sacrificing our time, energy, and money.

God has revealed Himself to us, and we have rejected Him. The only hope we have is found in Jesus, the name by which we are saved (John 14:6, Acts 4:12). If we assume that those who never hear the gospel will go to heaven because of their ignorance, then we would make all efforts to avoid their hearing, lest they be given a chance to reject the gospel and be condemned. Yet, in Scripture, we are commanded otherwise. We are told to go to the ends of the earth proclaiming the good news, persuading and leading as many to Christ as we can. It is an urgent mission of utmost importance. We have been called to share the gospel, and He is worthy of our love and obedience.

daily QUESTIONS

The gospel transforms not only our spiritual lives but also the hope we have every day. How has your life changed because of the gospel, and how does this inspire you to share the gospel with others?

Read Romans 9:2-3 and Romans 10:1. Do you feel this same burden for the lost in your life? If not, pray and ask that God would give you Paul's heart for the lost.

Which calls feel strongest in your life in your mission to share the gospel — the call from above, below, within, or beside?

"We have been called to share the gospel, and He is worthy of our love and obedience."

The Four Calls of Evangelism

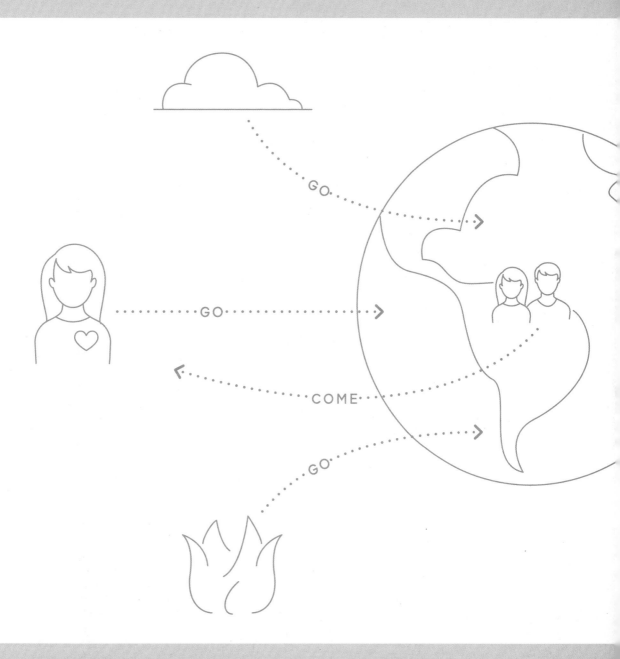

"*The world is watching to see if our faith is real.*"

Paul's Example

|

READ ACTS 16:11-40

"Expect great things from God. Attempt great things for God."

WILLIAM CAREY

Acts 16 shares the stories of three very different individuals who all encountered Christ. These unlikely characters—a wealthy woman, a demon-possessed slave, and a jailer—met Paul in the city of Philippi in three drastically different ways. As Paul shared the gospel with them, he modeled that evangelism is more than a method. He was sensitive to where the Spirit was working and shared the gospel in different ways with different people. He was also ready to share the gospel no matter where he was and no matter the cost because he knew that the gospel changes everything.

First, in Philippi, Paul encountered Lydia, a wealthy businesswoman. Lydia was a seller of purple cloths, which would have been an expensive and prestigious market at the time as the color purple was often associated with royalty. She was also a religious woman, likely a Gentile who believed in God but had not yet converted to Christianity. Paul met Lydia while she was at a prayer meeting outside the city gates. Though she sought God, she did not yet know the full gospel. As Paul shared about Jesus's life, death, and resurrection, her heart was opened. She believed in the good news and was immediately baptized. Lydia then invited Paul to stay at her home, which eventually became the church's meeting place in Philippi.

Another day, while Paul and Silas were going back to the prayer meeting, he met a demon-possessed slave girl. She was clairvoyant, and her owners would sell her as a fortune teller. This particular day, as the girl saw Paul and his companions, she started shouting, "These men, who are proclaiming to you the way of salvation, are the servants of the Most High God" (Acts 16:17). Paul became so bothered at her yelling that he looked at her and said, "I command you in the name of Jesus Christ to come out of her!" Immediately, the demonic spirit left her. Her owners, who saw that the girl would no longer produce an income for them, were furious at Paul. They invented false accusations against Paul and Silas and had them thrown in jail.

While in jail, Paul and Silas met the final character, the Philippian jailer. After being falsely condemned, Paul and Silas were thrown into a dungeon-like prison, reserved for the worst of criminals. Their feet were put in wooden stocks that were often used as torture devices. Even despite such horrific conditions, Paul and Silas spent the night singing and praying to the Lord. Around midnight, God released their chains by sending an earthquake. The doors to the prison opened, but remarkably, they chose to remain in the jail cell. When the guard woke up and saw the open gates, he grabbed his sword to kill himself, thinking that the prisoners had escaped on his watch. Paul quickly told him that the prisoners were all still there, and the guard ran over, fell to his knees. He said, "Sirs, what must I do to be saved?" And they responded, "Believe in the Lord Jesus, and you will be saved—you and your household" (Acts 16:30-31).

These three different individuals—each with different backgrounds, baggage, and beliefs—all encountered the gospel through Paul. Paul was ready to share the gospel, whether in prayer meetings or prison, and he prayed for the strength to do so boldly (Ephesians 6:19-20). From these stories, we can learn about the God who saves and how we can be ministers of His gospel.

Lydia's conversion story may seem the simplest and most desired example as we seek to evangelize. She was already interested in religion and had a heart to please God. However, she did not understand the full gospel. Paul simply shared from the Scriptures about who God is and what He has done. He invited Lydia to repent and believe, and she was saved. Sometimes we can also encounter people who are hungry to hear the good news of Christ. Perhaps they are already interested in religion or have been exploring the idea of a creator. As they hear the message of the gospel, their hearts are open, and they are saved.

Or perhaps we may meet someone similar to the slave girl. As readers, we do not know whether or not the slave girl became a follower of Jesus. Similarly, as we share the gospel, we may not know if the seed we plant will bear fruit in the years to come. Often it can take many years for a person to turn to Christ, and some people must hear the gospel dozens of times before they finally believe it and are saved. We may be called to share about Jesus with those who cannot hear the gospel clearly because of physical, emotional, or spiritual needs. They may be angry or antagonistic to the gospel because of abuse, hurt, or tragedy. While we are sharing the gospel in word, we must be sensitive to their barriers to the gospel and seek to bring the hope of the gospel in word and deed.

Finally, we may have the opportunity to bring the hope of the gospel through our suffering, as Paul and Silas did in prison. Paul was willing to suffer for the gospel and remained in the jail, even though the gates were opened for him. He was willing to give up his comfort, and even his own life, for the sake of making the gospel of Jesus known. In our suffering, we are given the same opportunity. In moments of trouble, whether with cancer or persecution, the world is watching to see if our faith is real. In these times, we are given the chance to point to the hope we have in Christ, even through our pain. By doing so, we are proclaiming the sufficiency of Christ in all seasons in our lives.

Read Acts 16:11-40. How does Paul share the gospel differently with each person?

_____

_____

_____

_____

_____

_____

_____

_____

_____

Have you seen God use suffering in your life as a witness to others?

_____

_____

_____

_____

_____

_____

_____

God can save all kinds of people—rich, poor, proud, and selfish. Is there any person in your life who you think is "beyond God's reach"? Spend time praying for that person in light of today's lesson.

_____

_____

_____

_____

_____

_____

_____

"We are given the chance to point to the hope we have in Christ, even through our pain. By doing so, we are proclaiming the sufficiency of Christ in all seasons in our lives."

The Gospel

BUT CHRIST BORE THE FULL WEIGHT
OF OUR SIN ON THE CROSS SO THAT
ALL WHO BELIEVE WILL RECEIVE
HIS RIGHTEOUSNESS.

*For God loved the world in this way: He gave his one and
only Son, so that everyone who believes in him will not
perish but have eternal life.*

John 3:16

OUR BROKENNESS AND SIN
NATURE SEPARATE US FROM
THE ONE TRUE, HOLY GOD.

for the wages of sin is death
Romans 6:23a

WHEN WE ACCEPT THE FREE
GIFT OF SALVATION, WE ARE
RECONCILED TO GOD AND
GIVEN ETERNAL LIFE.

*But to all who did receive him, he gave
them the right to be children of God,
to those who believe in his name*
John 1:12

"...*she knew her mission was not to win man's approval but God's.*"

72

Missionary Biographies, *Part 1*

READ 2 CORINTHIANS 5:14-20

"To know the will of God we need an open Bible and open map."

WILLIAM CAREY

Christian history is full of inspiring examples of men and women who gave up everything for the sake of sharing the gospel. Like Paul, they considered their lives "of no value to [themselves]" but considered it their purpose "to finish [their] course and the ministry [they] received from the Lord Jesus, to testify to the gospel of God's grace" (Acts 20:24). They gave up modern comforts, typical Christmas traditions, and, at times, even their own lives for the sake of sharing the gospel.

What could lead a man or a woman to sell all they have and go to the ends of the earth to share the gospel? Only the grace of God and a vision from Scripture to make Him known to the ends of the earth can compel one to act in such a way. As we study missionary biographies, it can be tempting to think, "I could never be like them!" Yet, most of these men and women started as ordinary believers, following God in the next step of obedience as He led them. They were not instant missionaries, nor were they the most qualified, sociable, or equipped. They were everyday men and women who chose to follow the call to share the gospel.

Consider, for example, the story of William Carey. Trained as a shoemaker in England, he worked as a cobbler and was known as a "poor-journeyman shoemaker." As a young pastor in England, he became burdened for the lost around the world. Despite opposition from fellow countrymen who did not see a need to share the gospel with others, he went to India as a missionary. Though he saw no conversions for seven years, he faithfully persevered.

Eventually, many came to faith in India. Carey also translated the Bible into many Indian dialects and founded a college to train local ministers. He lost two wives while in India and suffered other great personal losses. Though not a perfect evangelist, man, or father, God used him to bring many to Himself, and he is now known as the "father of modern missions" in India.

Or consider the story of Amy Carmichael, a young Irish woman who left Europe to minister to the "untouchables," the lowest caste in India. In her youth, Amy was a vivacious young girl who would often get in trouble for playing tricks at school, but when her father went bankrupt and died, she was forced to drop out of school and take care of her mother. She had no global ambitions at the time, but a few years later, she became burdened for the lost and went to Japan to share the gospel.

However, her missionary journey was not linear and without trial. Amy was forced to come back quickly from Japan because of chronic illness. She was torn, feeling a call to do mission work but unable to fulfill it due to the frailty of her physical body. In 1895, though, she was told that India might have a better climate for her illness, and she quickly boarded a ship to Bangalore. Little did she know that she would never return to Europe. She ministered for 55 years in India without a furlough.

Though she never married or had biological children, she became the mother of over a thousand young girls whom she rescued from being temple prostitutes and adopted into her care. At that time in India, poor young girls were often sold to Hindu priests to be married and usually ended up as temple prostitutes. One young girl named Preena tried to run away from this kind of life but was caught and branded with a hot iron. Once back at the temple, she remembered hearing about Amy, who would welcome the outcast into her home. Preena risked running away once more, this time to Amy's front door. As expected, Amy accepted young Preena into her home, though she could have been charged and put in jail for doing so. Soon, children by the dozens started being dropped off at Amy's door by destitute parents. As she continued to rescue these young children, she became well-known in her city and was not allowed to enter the temples freely. That did not stop her. Instead, she began to dye her hair and stain her skin with tea bags or coffee so that she could blend in and enter unnoticed into the temples.

Amy's life was not an easy one. Due to her chronic illness, she was often constrained to her bed for weeks at a time. For the final twenty years of her life, Amy was bedridden as a result of a fall. Despite her many physical challenges, she devoted her life to sharing the gospel through writing and continued rescuing society's vulnerable. Amy's ministry came at a cost relationally as well, as even her own missionary community could not understand her ministering to the lowest caste in Indian culture. The caste system combined with British imperial rule were strong in India, and most missionaries would not dare adopt Indian customs or minister to the lowest castes. Even so, Amy faithfully preached the message of the gospel in word and deed, sharing the truth of the gospel message while protecting the most vulnerable around her. She preserved through fear, conflict, illness, and division because she knew her mission was not to win man's approval but God's.

William Carey and Amy Carmichael were two missionaries who God used to bring many to faith in India. They surrendered their lives to the purpose of knowing God and making Him known. Like the faithful saints before us, let us share the gospel with others, risking rejection and reputation, not only because the need is great but because our God is worthy of worship.

Consider 2 Corinthians 5:14-20. What could compel people to leave their homes, comfort, and safety to share the gospel with others who are different from them?

_____

_____

_____

_____

_____

_____

_____

How do the lives of Amy Carmichael and William Carey encourage you to be faithful in sharing the gospel in your context?

_____

_____

_____

_____

_____

_____

_____

As believers, we are told to let our light shine before men, not hiding our faith even when it may cost us (Matthew 5:16). What holds you back from doing this?

_____

_____

_____

_____

_____

_____

_____

"*How can people be saved if no one preaches the gospel to them?*"

Missionary Biographies, *Part 2*

"He is no fool who gives what he cannot keep to gain what he cannot lose."

JIM ELLIOT

Reading the biographies of missionaries may leave us feeling either inspired or inadequate. Although their stories may sound incredible and unachievable, these men and women were regular people who simply obeyed the call. They were not instantly effective evangelists but instead worked hard to learn new languages, enter into foreign cultures, and love the people around them. They did not start off as Christian heroes, nor were their lives perfect. Each struggled against sin, and many even went years without seeing fruit for their full-time efforts. Their lives point not to their incredible skills or talents but to the One who is worthy of all worship. As we continue to read the following missionaries' stories, may we worship our great God, who uses ordinary, fallen men and women for His great purposes.

In recent years, Jim and Elisabeth Elliot's story has inspired many because of their willingness to go to a hostile people group in Ecuador. Jim was eventually killed by the same people he served, leaving behind his wife and young daughter, Valerie. After his death, Elisabeth took her daughter and went to live among her husband's killers, learning the language and sharing the gospel with them. Elisabeth forsook her modern comforts and safety, living among murderers and hours away from medical care, sleeping next to poisonous snakes, and bathing in rivers with unknown creatures. She did all of this in order to share the good news of the gospel with people whose ears it had never reached.

George Mueller is another remarkable story of God's grace. Born in Prussia, George was a troubled child who regularly lied to and stole from those around him. At ten years old, George's father sent him to live at the church in order to become a Lutheran clergyman. At the time, becoming a clergyman was considered a respectable career path, and his father wanted to give George a comfortable life within the church. Though young George studied by day, he played cards, gambled, drank, and escaped into bars at night. While confessing to the priest, he would not only withhold his sins but would also steal the money his father had given him to tithe. At sixteen years old, he was caught stealing from a hotel and put in jail, but even after his imprisonment, he showed no repentance or desire to please God. He continued his religious studies and went to divinity school but continued to steal, lie, and indulge in every worldly pleasure, thinking little of God.

One day, a fellow divinity student, who also lived George's lifestyle, told George about a Christian Bible study happening on campus. Inexplicably, George knew he had to attend. When he heard the Word shared and the prayers prayed, he felt a happiness he had not known in all his years of pleasure-seeking. He repented of his sins and gave up his path of open, habitual rebellion. He wanted to become a missionary and wrote to his family, telling them of the happiness he had found. He encouraged his family to seek the Lord too to find peace and joy. Instead of celebration, he received only an angry letter from his family in return. Becoming a missionary was not the comfortable life his father had imagined for him. Because of his age, George could only become a missionary with his father's approval, which he could not obtain. So instead, George passed out thousands of tracts and began sharing the gospel wherever he went.

Several years later, George was finally able to become a missionary to the Jews in London. He continued to work throughout England but began to feel convicted that he should not receive a salary for his pastoral work. He continued to serve, accepting only unsolicited donations, and eventually established several orphanages in the area. Throughout his lifetime, George cared for over 10,000 orphans. Even though he built several buildings and cared for thousands of children, he never made his financial needs known to man, presenting them only to the Father. Through prayer, George Mueller saw God provide abundantly. For example, one morning at the orphanage, three hundred children had nothing to eat. They sat down at breakfast time and prayed when suddenly there was a knock at the door. The local baker had felt compelled to bring the kids dozens of loaves of bread. At the same time, the local dairy farmer showed up, saying that his cart had broken down in front of the orphanage. Not able to make his deliveries, he gave the milk to the children who feasted and rejoiced in God's provision for them. Over his life, he raised over four hundred thousand pounds, the equivalent of roughly seven million dollars today. This man, who had been a liar and a thief, surrendered his life to the Lord and worked faithfully to share the gospel around the world despite his physical weakness.

With each of these missionaries, their vision was clear. How can people be saved if no one preaches the gospel to them? They knew their life on Earth was temporary and an offering to the Lord and prepared for the eternal home that awaited them. Throughout the Scriptures, we also find examples of "heroes of the faith," men and women who were once liars, adulterers, prostitutes, and murderers, who surrendered their lives to God (Hebrews 11). These believers were not righteous on their own but because of the extravagant grace of God. Perhaps because of these very sins, they knew of their need for a Savior whose righteousness far exceeded their own. Once saved, they gave up comfort, stability, and even their own lives for the purpose of making God known. They knew this home was not their own and longed for a better country — a heavenly one. "Therefore, God is not ashamed to be called their God, for he has prepared a city for them" (Hebrews 11:16). Like the imperfect men and women before us, may we seek to do the same, faithfully obeying the Lord in each new step He sets before us.

daily QUESTIONS

Read Mark 10:29-30. Is following Jesus worth it to you, even if you lose everything (friendships, relationships, housing, or even your life)?

_____

_____

_____

_____

_____

What weaknesses or excuses have you used to keep you from faithfully sharing your faith?
How do the stories of these missionaries inspire you to be faithful to God's call in evangelism?

_____

_____

_____

_____

_____

Spend time praying for unreached people groups around the world. The Joshua Project is a great place to learn about these groups who have little to no access to the gospel. Download the app on your phone, or go to the website today and pray for the unreached people group of the day.

Therefore, since we also have such a large cloud of witnesses surrounding us, let us lay aside every hindrance and the sin that so easily ensnares us. Let us run with endurance the race that lies before us.

HEBREWS 12:1

weekly REFLECTION

Review all Scripture passages from the week.

Summarize the main points from this week's Scripture readings.

_____   _____
_____   _____
_____   _____
_____   _____
_____   _____
_____   _____
_____   _____
_____   _____

What did you observe from this week's passages about God and His character?

_____
_____
_____
_____
_____
_____

What do this week's passages reveal about the condition of mankind and yourself?

_____
_____
_____
_____

How do these passages point to the gospel?

_____

_____

_____

_____

_____

How should you respond to these Scriptures? What specific action steps
can you take this week to apply them in your life?

_____

_____

_____

_____   _____

_____   _____

_____   _____

_____   _____

Write a prayer in response to your study of God's Word. Adore God for who He is,
confess sins He revealed in your own life, ask Him to empower you to walk in obedience,
and pray for anyone who comes to mind as you study.

_____

_____

_____

_____

_____

_____

_____

_____

"We must let the gospel's message define us."

How to Share the Gospel

|

READ ACTS 28

"I cannot tell you what joy it gave me to bring the first soul to the Lord Jesus Christ. I have tasted almost all the pleasures that this world can give. I do not suppose there is one that I have not experienced, but I can tell you that those pleasures were as nothing compared to the joy that the saving of that one soul gave me."

C.T. STUDD

In evangelism, our theology should drive our methodology. In other words, what we believe should inform how we behave. This is why we spent the first two weeks of this study discussing the theology of evangelism, namely what the gospel is and why we share it. Now, over the next several weeks, we will review our methodology. How do we share the gospel? How do we transition to the gospel in conversations? These methods will become like tools in your toolbox, but they are by no means exhaustive. There is no "one size fits all" evangelism method, just as no two people are the same. We see this in the New Testament as the disciples used parables, miracles, stories, songs, and letters to share the gospel. Each person with whom we share may indeed have different questions about life, including:

- *What is the meaning of my life?*
- *How do I face death?*
- *What is my identity?*
- *How do I handle suffering?*
- *How can I be happy?*

The message, not the method, is what makes this evangelism. While a conversation may look different based on each individual's background, the message of Jesus's life, death, and resurrection remain the same. Still, there are a few general principles that can help you share the gospel, including the following plan of action:

PRAY

God is the one who saves. As we seek to share the gospel, we should begin by praying for opportunities, boldness, and clarity. We can also pray that God would open the eyes of the person we are talking to in order that he or she can be saved.

LOVE

We share the gospel out of love for God and others. We are not seeking sneaky evangelistic opportunities or trying to trick people into following Jesus. Instead, we are to truly love those around us, being involved in the hundreds of conversations that make up day-to-day experiences, getting to know those around us, and expressing genuine interest in their lives.

OBSERVE

Ask good questions, and become a conversationalist. Observe what is important to others and what they value. For example, if you are in someone's home, notice that person's pictures, decorations, and interests, and ask about them. Look for areas of common ground, and agree where you can. Be prepared to talk about surface-level topics (i.e., decorating, the weather, and their kid's sleeping patterns), so that they feel loved and trust you when you bridge into deeper, worldview conversations.

As you observe and listen throughout the conversation, look for a bridge to deeper conversations. Ask about someone's story, and be a good listener. As you spend time with someone, inevitably, you will find something that is broken because of the fall. Note that many people feel more comfortable talking about deeper worldviews and faith-based topics in private, so if possible, make a plan to invite your friend to coffee or dessert at your house.

INITIATE SPIRITUAL CONVERSATIONS

Use questions to transition to spiritual conversations, and be prepared to share the gospel with them. We will discuss examples to bridge into spiritual conversations in the following weeks, but as you engage in spiritual conversation, remain focused on the gospel. It is easy to become caught up in secondary, controversial issues, but we must let the gospel's message define us, not our stance on politics or schooling decisions. Also, remember that you do not need to have the answer to every question or know all that there is to know about Christianity. Share what you know, and be willing to say, "I do not know, but I will look it up and get back to you." This does not need to be overly formal or polished; rather, the goal is to engage in spiritual conversations personally and simply.

ASK FOR
A RESPONSE

After you have shared spiritual truth, it is helpful to hear what the other person thinks about it. Ask questions like, "What do you think about that? Have you ever heard this before?" Sometimes as we ask these questions, it may become obvious that there are additional objections that the person may have to the gospel. Or, perhaps there is something that we did not explain clearly. This is a great opportunity to let the other person engage with what we just said—remembering that in order for someone to be saved, that person must respond to the message of the gospel.

PRAY

Before we share, as we share, and after we share, we must pray. The Lord is the one who saves, and He can use whomever He chooses. He can use the most babbling, rambling, and inadequate of conversations to bring someone to faith. While we can be used in this amazing mission, we must remain close to the source, our Father.

When we share the gospel, we seek to pray, love, observe, transition to spiritual conversation, and ask for a response. As we do this, we must remain sensitive to the Spirit, seeking to love and engage in meaningful conversations with those around us. In each evangelistic opportunity, we are joyfully able to invite others to the life-changing hope found in Christ.

IN EACH EVANGELISTIC OPPORTUNITY, WE ARE JOYFULLY ABLE TO INVITE OTHERS TO THE LIFE-CHANGING HOPE FOUND IN CHRIST.

Which of the six steps do you most often forget? Which step is hardest for you?

_____

_____

_____

_____

_____

_____

_____

Consider Acts 28. How and where does Paul share the gospel in these verses?

_____

_____

_____

_____

_____

_____

_____

What characteristics define Paul's evangelism?

_____

_____

_____

_____

_____

_____

_____

_____

Steps for Evangelism

PRAY

LOVE

OBSERVE

INITIATE SPIRITUAL
CONVERSATION

ASK FOR A
RESPONSE

PRAY

"Sharing your testimony is a great way to talk about your Savior."

Personal Testimony

|

READ ACTS 9:1-19

"The Great Commission says to make disciples, not get followers.
There is a difference."

MIGUEL NUNEZ

The word "testimony" means "a witness or public declaration of the truth." Throughout the Bible, many men and women gave testimonies of the Lord's salvation, including David, Hannah, and Mary. As they proclaimed God's work in their lives, they welcomed others to worship Him too. As Christians, we each have a unique testimony of how God saved us. When we share our testimonies, we invite listeners to view the world as we do through storytelling. We share how we see life and bid that our listeners consider the possibility of God, sin, and Christ in the world. We tell stories of God's goodness in our lives, and like the blind man in John 9:25, we can proclaim, "I was blind, and now I can see!"

The Apostle Paul also shared his testimony as a key element in his evangelism. In the book of Acts, Paul shared his personal testimony on three different accounts:

- *Acts 9: Paul described the events of his conversion when they happened.*

- *Acts 22: Paul was falsely accused and on trial before the Jews.*
  He spoke to the people about who God is and how Jesus saved Paul.

- *Acts 26: After Paul was imprisoned for over a year, he met with the Judean king.*
  He shared his conversion experience and invited the king to believe in Jesus.

Paul, who had been killing Christians, used his past to point to the incredible, miraculous work of God's salvation. His testimony reminds us that our broken past is not too sinful to share with others. Rather, it can be a useful tool to display God's greatness—that He would save sinners like us. When sharing our testimonies, we can be honest with our stories, magnifying not ourselves but the One who saved us.

When we share our testimonies, we may also choose to contextualize based on who our listeners are. In all three examples in Acts, Paul shared the story of how God saved him, yet he also included specific details that were fitting for his listeners. While keeping the key narrative of his salvation the same, he contextualized and included details that were uniquely suited for his hearers at the time. Based on who you are sharing with, you may also choose to include different details of your life. If you are sharing with a student, for example, you may emphasize your life in school. Or, if you are sharing with a Muslim, you may emphasize how you tried to follow all the rules. You are not changing the substance of how God saved you but are emphasizing specific details of your story based on who you are telling.

Just as with Paul's examples, most testimonies include before, during, and after sections. Use the following prompts to think about your testimony, and write them in the corresponding worksheet page found on page 95.

BEFORE

What was your life like before you were saved? What were some of your thoughts and feelings from this season? What did you do to seek happiness, fulfillment, and love? How did you view your identity? What were some of the difficulties in your life that led you to turn to Christ?

If you were saved while you were a small child, you might not remember your life before Christ. If this is your story, share it honestly. You can talk of being saved as a young child while also mentioning any struggles you may have had since then and how the Lord has helped you in trials. As you share your story, speak truthfully, and look for opportunities to bridge to the other person's experience if possible. For example, if you know that you and your listener both struggled with an eating disorder or addiction, make sure to include those details as a part of your story.

DURING

When did God save you? What is the gospel, and why did you believe it? Who shared the gospel with you?

During the middle section of your testimony, clearly share the truth of the gospel. What is the gospel? When did you first hear the gospel? How long did it take for you to repent of your sins and turn to Christ? Sometimes it can be hard to identify the specific moment when you were saved. Perhaps it was after a long season of wrestling with God. If this is your story, share what you remember, narrowing in on a few specific details. Discuss the driving factors that led you to stop trusting in your own works and trust in Christ's. If you are unsure how and when God saved you, use this as a chance to reflect. Have you ever repented of your sins and believed in the finished work of Christ? It is never too late! As we share the story of how God saved us, it is not only helpful for those listening but also for ourselves as it reminds us of the great mercy that God has shown to us.

How has your life changed since you became a follower of Christ? How has your hope, joy, or peace been altered?

Mention a few specific examples of ways your life has changed since you were saved. You do not need to paint a perfect picture of life, but this is a great opportunity to point to the transformative power of God, not only for eternity but also for our day-to-day lives. Speak honestly of the hope, joy, and peace you have found in Christ.

As you share your testimony, you are inviting the listener to see how you view the world. Remember that the person you are sharing your story with may not have the same religious background as you and may not understand words such as "gospel," "redeemed," or "sin." Avoid overly-Christian terms unless you know your listener will understand them. Explain ideas, and define terms simply rather than using religious words to communicate your story.

Your story is unique, and people want to hear a good narrative. It is hard to refute a story about your life, and sharing your testimony is a great way to talk about your Savior and naturally share the gospel.

We tell stories of God's goodness in our lives, and like the blind man in John 9:25, we can proclaim, "I was blind, and now I can see!"

Read Revelation 12:10-11. One day when Christ defeats Satan, we will live with Him forever. What role does our testimony play in these verses?

_____

_____

_____

_____

_____

_____

_____

_____

_____

_____

Read Paul's three testimonies, and note any differences in the details included. What do you learn about contextualization from Paul's example?

_____

_____

_____

_____

_____

_____

_____

_____

_____

_____

Write out your testimony using the worksheet on the next page.

Crafting Your Personal Testimony

Use this space to write out your testimony. If possible, share this with someone from your church, and ask for their feedback. Exchanging testimonies can be a great exercise not only for practice but also as an encouragement as you reflect on the Lord's work in your life.

What was your life like before Christ? (Try to focus on a few key points.)

_____

_____

_____

_____

How did you encounter Christ? Who told you about the gospel, and what was your response? (Make sure to include the four points of the gospel from page 59 in your response.)

_____

_____

_____

_____

_____

_____

How has your life changed since you were saved? Include one or two specific examples of how you have seen God at work in your life.

_____

_____

_____

_____

_____

"Hospitality is both an art and a science."

Hospitality

"There is no need for faith where there is no consciousness of an element of risk."

ELISABETH ELLIOT

In Greek, the word "hospitality" means "love of strangers." Throughout Scripture, it was assumed that when we follow God, we will love others by inviting them into our lives and homes. Hospitality is not meant to be an exceptional part of the Christian experience but a normative one. When we practice hospitality, we put the gospel on display as we invite the lonely, the outsider, and the broken into our families. We gather them in close and care for their needs. We invest in our local communities. And as we do this, we remember that we, too, were once lonely outsiders who were separated from God. Just as God invited us to feast at His table while we were still His enemies, so we too are to love others.

As we practice hospitality, we spend our time, money, and talents on others. We balance our budget to include providing meals for others, and we allocate our time to love and serve them. This concept of hospitality is very different from entertaining. When we show biblical hospitality, we do not seek to put on a show or make ourselves look good. We do not seek compliments on our home decorating skills or try to draw attention to ourselves. We do not pick expensive meals so that others will think highly of us. Instead, we aim to make our homes inviting to others by cleaning and offering our best out of love for them. We dine with those who do not look like us, think like us, or behave like us. We invite others into our homes, not out of selfish ambition but out of love for God and others.

When we love strangers, we affirm that every person is made in God's image. As we get to know our guests, we share our lives with them. We are involved in normal day-to-day conversations and are ready to share about God naturally as the most important thing in our lives. We share stories of grace and invite them into family rhythms. We speak kindly and listen well. We become students, remembering what our guests like and do not like, their allergies, and pets' names. We ask good questions and seek bridges to spiritual conversations.

Sometimes, we may hesitate to invite those who are not like us into our homes. We may be afraid that our differences will provoke conflict, or we may be afraid of their sin. It is important to remember that we can love others without always agreeing with them. Jesus modeled this for us, eating and drinking with people who were unlike Him—with the broken, drunkards, and prostitutes. As we pray for our neighbors and get to know them, we treat them less as caricatures, assuming what they think. We do not need to attack them for their sin, nor do we affirm it. We love them where they are, sharing the hope that we have with truth and grace.

Hospitality is also a great way to invite someone into your family's rhythms. As such, we must be spiritually prepared, rooted in the Word, active in prayer, and involved in our local churches. When we host others, we naturally display whatever is in our hearts. If we are in the pattern of praying before meals, for example, we can easily invite others to join us. Or, if we have family devotions after dinner or pray with our children before bed, we can invite our guests to join along. If you do not already implement regular family devotions, today is a great day to start them!

CONSIDER THESE PRACTICAL TIPS ON HOSPITALITY:

- *Prayerfully make a list of people you would like to invite to your home.*

- *Budget for hospitality, and plan for it in your calendar.*

- *Develop a list of easy hospitality meals, like tacos, lasagna, or sheet-pan meals.*

- *Invite your guests to your home. An easy place to start is by inviting someone over for coffee or dessert.*

- *Ask good questions, and be a good listener.*

- *Pray before someone comes over to your home. Pray for their hearts and for yours. Pray they would feel loved, for opportunities to share the gospel, and the boldness to take them.*

- *Remember that you are hosting people who need to be rescued from their sin, not be lectured on the importance of secondary issues, like politics or organic food. Your guest may say offensive statements or act in a way that is not culturally sensitive. Learn to love and forgive quickly, even when they do not ask for your forgiveness.*

- *Ask to hear their story. If they ask about your story, be ready to share your testimony.*

- *Be in the Word, active in prayer, and involved in your local church.*

Hospitality is both an art and a science. As you host others, you will learn what works well for your family's rhythms and personality. We need not worry about having a spotless house or a designer kitchen, but rather we can focus on loving God and others with our time, talents, and treasures. As we prayerfully invite others to enjoy our food and fellowship, we are not seeking sneaky evangelistic conversations but are seeking to boldly share our lives with our guests in love, which includes the hope we have found in the gospel.

daily QUESTIONS

Consider Genesis 18:1-8, Romans 12:13, and Hebrews 13:2. How does hospitality mark the lives of believers throughout the Bible?

Make a list of people for whom you would like to show hospitality — text one person from your list to invite them over for coffee, dinner, or dessert. Make your grocery list, and budget accordingly.

Read Proverbs 14:31. How can you be generous to those in need through hospitality?

Reading the Bible
with Someone

If someone is open to spiritual conversations, invite that person to read the
Bible with you. To do this, you may say something like, "Have you ever read
the Bible? Would you like to read it and talk about it together, kind of like
a book club?" or "We have talked some about Jesus, but have you ever read
His claims firsthand? I would want to read it for myself to formulate my own
opinions about who He is based on what He said and did." Or you may say
something like, "The Bible is the most famous book of all time, and Jesus is
the most controversial teacher. Would you like to know what it says?"

When you get together, take turns reading chapters of Scripture out
loud, and let the Bible drive the conversation, asking questions like:

- What did you think of the chapter?

- What was confusing?

- What did this reading teach you
  about who God is?

- What does it teach you about man?

- What does it teach you about how God
  relates with man?

- Is there anything you learned or think you
  should do because of what you read?

- Is the God of the Bible who you
  expected Him to be?

MARK IS THE SHORTEST OF THE GOSPELS AND CAN BE AN EXCELLENT PLACE TO START.

If your friend has never read the Bible before, help her find the book of Mark, and explain what the Bible is about in a sentence or two. For example, you may share that the Bible is God's Word and that it is one big story about who God is and how we can be right with Him. As you are talking, remember that many people do not know Christian words such as "repentance," "glorify," or "sanctification." Use words that are simple to understand, and explain terms as appropriate.

IF POSSIBLE, PREPARE BY READING THE CHAPTER AHEAD OF TIME AND LOOKING THROUGH A GOOD STUDY BIBLE TO ANTICIPATE ANY QUESTIONS.

If your friend asks a question that you do not know the answer to, do not make it up. Simply say, "I do not know. That is a great question!" and look up the answer later. We are all still growing in our knowledge of God, and showing humility is better than faking knowledge.

AS YOU FINISH YOUR TIME, ASK IF YOU CAN PRAY FOR YOUR FRIEND.

Usually, even non-religious people will accept prayer from what they view as a "spiritual" person. Before you leave, set a time to get together again to read the next chapter. Throughout the week, pray for God to work in your friend's heart to bring repentance and faith.

"The key to Bible storying is to know the Bible well."

Bible Storying

READ ACTS 7:1-54

"Go, send, or disobey."

JOHN PIPER

WHAT IS BIBLE STORYING?

Bible storying is telling the stories of the Bible in an accessible way. Sometimes when we share the gospel, we do not want to interrupt the conversation to look up a story or a verse from the Bible. Instead, we can have Bible stories memorized and share them naturally in conversation. Similar to your personal testimony, telling Bible stories can be a great way to invite your listener to consider your worldview in a disarming way.

Historically, Bible storying has often been used in missionary settings. Stories are exchanged among different people groups, and the message of the gospel is shared in narrative form. Today in the West, the need for Bible storying is increasing as a growing percentage of adults are now biblically illiterate. They have never heard of the stories of Jesus and do not know what the Bible says.

HOW TO TELL A BIBLE STORY

The key to Bible storying is to know the Bible well. We cannot share stories that we do not know. Study a story beforehand so that you understand its details and can stay biblically accurate. You do not need to include every detail of the story, but be sure to remain accurate in the message and details you include. We do not want to add to or embellish the Bible.

Through Bible storying, we tell Bible stories in as much detail as possible and in a dynamic and expressive manner. As you share these stories, use facial expressions, emotions, and body language to help you communicate. If you are speaking of Jesus healing a sick boy, for example, remember that this is a miraculous and wonderful story! Try to express this truth with excitement in your voice and on your face. Think through the story from your listener's perspective, and explain any ideas that are difficult to understand without previous biblical knowledge, such as a spiritual sacrifice or a traditional marriage custom.

As you share stories from the Bible, draw out the gospel's main points: God, sin, Jesus, and response. For example, in the Old Testament, we can point to God, who created and sustains all, or describe men or women's sinfulness. We explain how the brokenness, failures, or victories of men and women in the Bible point to the need for the Savior. We can share stories about what Jesus said and did or how men and women responded to Him.

CHOOSING SUITABLE STORIES

If you think you may only have one conversation with someone, pick a story that allows you to present the gospel easily. If you have several weeks to talk with someone, you can go through the Bible at a slower pace. All of Scripture points to Jesus (Luke 24:25-27), so you can truly use any story to transition to the gospel.

You can also share the gospel in narrative form. As Sam Chan says, "When I have to give my own quick summary of the gospel, I use an outline, which I learned from Tim Keller. It's called Manger, Cross, and King. My main points will be: Jesus, the Son of God, came to us as a human. But the most amazing thing He did was to die for us on a cross. And one day Jesus will come again to set up His kingdom on earth."

To prepare, choose 5-10 Bible stories to share over several weeks. Based on your listener and frequency of conversation, you may choose to focus on the entire Bible or exclusively on stories of Jesus, picking 5-10 stories that magnify His power, love, or humility.

HERE ARE A FEW IDEAS FOR BIBLE STORIES:

- Creation Story: Genesis 1
- The Fall: Genesis 3
- Old Testament Men and Women:
  The call of Abraham: Genesis 12
  Abraham and Isaac: Genesis 22:1-19
  Joseph: Genesis 37-50
  Moses and the burning bush: Exodus 3:1-12
  The exodus of the Israelites from Egypt: Exodus 12:21-38, 14:1-31
  Hannah: 1 Samuel 1:1-20
- Stories about Jesus:
  Baptism of Jesus: Matthew 3:13-17
  Calling of the disciples: Matthew 4:18-22
  Healing of the blind man: John 9:1-41

  Jesus healing the bleeding woman: Mark 5:25-34
  Power over all creation: Matthew 8:23-34
  The raising of Lazarus: John 11:1-44
  How people responded to Jesus's miracles: Matthew 9:1-8
  Jesus's death: Matthew 27:32-56
  Jesus's resurrection: Luke 24

- The Early Church and Jesus's Second Return:
  Paul's conversion story: Acts 9
  Jesus is coming again: Revelation 22:6-21

- A Condensed Story from Creation to Christ: Genesis through Revelation

Bible storying can be a great way to share the gospel with kids. Kids have great imaginations and can typically identify with characters in stories. If you are sharing stories with kids, it can be fun to involve them in the storytelling process! For example, as you share:

1. *Share the story.*

2. *Ask them to help you tell it or act it out.*

3. *Have them share the story.*

When you have finished telling the story, ask questions like: What did you like about the story? Was there anything you did not like or that was confusing about the story? What do you think this story is telling you about Jesus? Stories about real people intrigue us and stay with us long after we hear them. As we narrate stories from the Bible, we share biblical truth in a disarming and natural way.

daily QUESTIONS

Throughout the Bible, stories were passed down from generation to generation. Consider Acts 7:1-54. How does Stephen's use of Bible storying effectively communicate his point?

_____

_____

_____

Identify 5-10 stories that you would like to study with a friend, and plan to review them this week.

_____

_____

_____

_____

Work through the Bible Storying Worksheet: Story of the Woman at the Well, which is located on page 106. Once you complete the worksheet, practice memorizing, and telling one Bible story.

Bible Storying Worksheet

STORY OF THE WOMAN AT THE WELL, JOHN 4

READ THE STORY OF JOHN 4:1-26 THREE TIMES.

The first time, read the story from start to finish.

The second time, read it from another translation if possible, and slow down to observe the details. Try to make a mental picture of what happened. Notice who the main characters are, where they were, who spoke, and what they said.

The third time, write down the key events of the story.

Who is the story about? _____

_____

Where does the story take place? _____

_____

What are the main characters doing? _____

_____

_____

_____

_____

_____

_____

Who speaks in the story, and what do they say?

_____

_____

_____

_____

_____

What details are included in the story?

_____

_____

_____

_____

What is the main point of the story?

_____

_____

Write the story from memory, including all of the details you can remember.

_____

_____

_____

_____

_____

_____

After you have written down these details, practice retelling the story with your Bible open in front of you to confirm any details. Then practice saying it with your Bible closed.

You are now ready to share the story with someone else! When you tell the story to someone, ask that person: *Have you ever heard this story before? What did you think about it?*

"Our strength is found in the unchanging kingdom of God."

Bridges and Contextualization

|

READ ACTS 17:16-34, 1 CORINTHIANS 9:19-23

> "Whatever we do, we must not treat the Great Commission like it's the Great Suggestion."
>
> CHARLES R. SWINDOLL

In Acts 17, Paul travels to the city of Athens to share the gospel. Athens was once known as the intellectual center of the world. It had a famous university, and the people loved hearing new ideas and debating religious theories. Though the city was declining, the people continued their spiritual debates and had idols for every human need.

When the people of Athens heard Paul speaking about Jesus in the city, they were curious about this new spiritual theology. They brought him to the religious council on the top of a hill to explain what he was saying. From the hilltop, Paul boldly proclaimed the message of the gospel. He found common ground with his listeners, used bridges to enter into gospel conversation, and contextualized to share the good news. As he did this, Paul identified problems within their worldview and presented the gospel as the solution.

COMMON GROUND

While in the town, Paul had observed the many traditions and idols of the people. There were gods of war, fertility, and love. He noticed that one of the idols had an inscription that read, "To an Unknown God" (Acts 17:23). Though the people did not yet believe in the gospel, Paul recognized that the men were "very religious" and valued spiritual conversation. This was common ground for them both.

BRIDGES

Paul used this common ground to bridge into gospel conversation. Using the idol to the unknown god as a launching point to the gospel, he proclaimed, "For as I was passing through and observing the objects of your worship, I even found an altar on which was inscribed, 'To an Unknown God.' Therefore, what you worship in ignorance, this I proclaim to you. The God who made the world and everything in it—he is Lord of heaven and earth—does not live in shrines made by hands" (Acts 17:23-24). Paul used this bridge to engage in spiritual conversation and identified a problem in their worldview. The people of Athens believed in a god they did not know. Paul had come to proclaim the one true God.

CONTEXTUALIZATION

Finally, Paul shared the gospel contextually. As Paul shared biblical truth, he shared it in a way that they would understand and used familiar ideas. Paul knew that his listeners were composed of both Stoics and Epicureans. Stoics of the day believed in reason, self-sufficiency, and obedience. For them, Paul emphasized God's sufficient character and the duty of man to repent and follow Him. Epicureans believed that pleasure and peace were the most important things in life, and they viewed gods as far-off beings who did not involve themselves with humans. For the Epicureans, Paul emphasized that God does exist, and He is close. He shared that God made us to know Him, but we have rebelled against Him. And to all, Paul appealed to the common idols of the day, using the word "life," which was particularly associated with the Greek god, Zeus, who was believed to rule many aspects of human life. Paul appealed to their religious history, affirming that God is the true giver of life.

As Paul contextualized, he did not water down the message of the gospel. He spoke clearly and boldly, knowing that he could be arrested or driven from the town, as had happened in two prior cities at the beginning of Acts 17. Despite these risks, Paul preserved by sharing the gospel in word and deed.

While Paul lived in the city, he did everything within his power to point to the truth of the gospel. He took care of his financial burdens so that his lifestyle did not deter people from believing in the gospel. He ate Greek food, spoke the local language, and used examples that they would understand. Paul entered into their world so that the gospel would be clearly communicated.

APPLICATION

Today, we can use the same spiritual strategy to share the gospel. Through bridges, common ground, and contextualization, we present the gospel in ways that our listeners will understand without watering down its message. We seek to be good listeners and observers of those around us, relating with them as possible. We find *common ground* in conversation, agreeing where we can.

As we find this common ground, we *identify bridges* to gospel conversation and identify problems in their worldviews. For instance, we may agree with another mom that we want happy, well-adjusted kids. We engage in conversations about schooling, after-school activities, and how to get into a good college. But as we speak, we also identify an underlying problem in this conversation. What about kids who are not happy, successful, or well-adjusted? Is there any hope for them? Or what if our children rebel against good parenting and do not turn out as we hope them to be? The hope of the gospel tells us that God did not come just for well-adjusted individuals. He loves the broken and downcast. He is with us even when our parenting fails or when our kids rebel. Christ came to bring a hope that surpasses all of our wildest hopes and dreams in parenting. This topic of motherhood becomes a bridge to an existential conversation, through which we can share the gospel *contextually*.

As another example, we may agree that the world is broken and that our country's political climate is divided. The problem here is easy to identify. What if our country never self-corrects and continues to become more and more hostile? Are politics really meant to satisfy or provide ultimate stability for our lives? In this conversation, we can point to our ultimate hope that is not rooted in political change. Our confidence is not rooted in a stable government; our strength is found in the unchanging kingdom of God. As Christians, we can have joy, regardless of our political leaders, because we identify with a kingdom that will never pass away. This, too, becomes a bridge to share the gospel.

As Paul found common ground, identified bridges, and used contextualization, he did not water down the message of the gospel. Rather, he sought to share the gospel in a bold and loving manner.

daily QUESTIONS

Re-read Acts 17:16-34. Underline the story's references to the four points of the gospel: God, sin, Christ, and response.

Make a list of 5-10 possible bridges to the gospel, such as politics, schooling, or marriage.

_____   _____

_____   _____

_____   _____

_____   _____

What are some problems you can identify in these worldview topics? How do these issues fall short of satisfying us, and how is the gospel the solution?

_____

_____

_____

_____

_____

_____

Finding Bridges

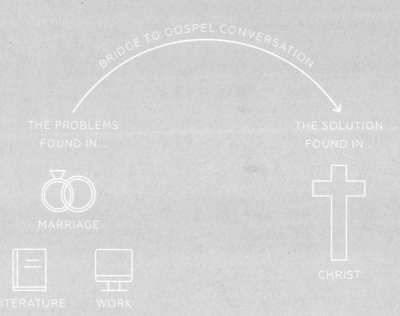

BRIDGE TO GOSPEL CONVERSATION

THE PROBLEMS FOUND IN...

THE SOLUTION FOUND IN...

MARRIAGE

LITERATURE   WORK

ARTS & CULTURE   PARENTING

TOPICS OF COMMON GROUND

CHRIST

Tips for Evangelism

Spiritual Tips for Evangelism

- Be in the Word, and pray daily.
- Have a clear understanding of the gospel.
- Be sensitive to the Spirit.
- Live a life of repentance, turning away from sin.
- Avoid gossip in order not to taint your witness.
- Persevere in prayer and evangelism.
- Be a part of a Bible-believing local church. If possible, invite another member into your relationships with non-believers, and partner to share the gospel together.
- Be content with your role. God may use you to plant a seed, while someone else may water it or see it grow.
- Rejoice when you begin to feel comfortable sharing the gospel with another!

Relational Tips for Evangelism

- Ask good questions.
- Be a good listener. Focus on what others are saying, not what you want to say back.
- Be friendly. Do not make people an evangelistic project. Be kind, and genuinely care about what they have to say.
- Observe body language.
- Speak kindly.
- Live a godly life. Your life and love will often trump what you say. Let it uphold your word and not disqualify it.
- Use what people say online as an opportunity to follow up privately, in person.
- Do not be afraid to say "I do not know."
- Be gracious, and do not assume you know what someone else thinks or believes.
- Stay focused on the gospel instead of other differences like politics or schooling decisions.

Then he said to his
disciples, "The harvest is
abundant, but the workers
are few. Therefore, pray
to the Lord of the harvest
to send out workers into
his harvest."

MATTHEW 9:37-38

weekly REFLECTION

Review all Scripture passages from the week.

Summarize the main points from this week's Scripture readings.

_____   _____
_____   _____
_____   _____
_____   _____
_____   _____
_____   _____
_____   _____
_____   _____
_____   _____
_____   _____

What did you observe from this week's passages about God and His character?

_____
_____
_____
_____
_____
_____
_____

What do this week's passages reveal about the condition of mankind and yourself?

_____
_____
_____
_____
_____

How do these passages point to the gospel?

_____

_____

_____

_____

_____

How should you respond to these Scriptures? What specific action steps
can you take this week to apply them in your life?

_____

_____

_____

_____   _____

_____   _____

_____   _____

_____   _____

Write a prayer in response to your study of God's Word. Adore God for who He is,
confess sins He revealed in your own life, ask Him to empower you to walk in obedience,
and pray for anyone who comes to mind as you study.

_____

_____

_____

_____

_____

_____

_____

_____

Introduction to Apologetics

Why do you believe what you believe? Why do you believe the world is round or the sun will come up tomorrow? Is it because you learned it as a child, or did you arrive at the conclusion rationally? Did someone you trust teach you these things, or, conversely, have you made conclusions about the way the world works through painful circumstances? We all have beliefs called plausibility structures. Plausibility structures are the structures we use to interpret meaning or the plausibility of something being true. And we all interpret external evidence around these structures. For example, you have likely not flown all around the world in order to prove that the world is round. Perhaps you have seen movies of spaceships or learned about the world in school. Maybe you were taught about the world through a trusted authority figure. Though you have not seen it firsthand, your belief that the world is round is based on other plausibility structures.

Whenever we learn something new, we learn through three categories: *logos, pathos, and ethos.* Usually, the information presented must make logical sense to us, appealing to our rational nature (*logos*). New facts or ideas must also appeal to us on an emotional level (*pathos*) for us to be compelled by them or at least guarantee that we do not have a strong emotional aversion to its message. Finally, we must trust the source giving us this information (*ethos*). When we evangelize, we seek to share the gospel using all three categories presented above.

In conversation, we must be good students of our friends or family members and determine the root of unbelief in our friends. Are our friends not becoming Christians because of a lack of information (*logos*) or because its teaching on homosexuality repulses them (*pathos*)? Do they not trust the authenticity of the Bible or its translations (*ethos*)? Or are they caught up with an emotional reserva-

66

We must be good students of our friends and family members and determine the root of unbelief.

tion, or have they been hurt in the past by some-one who called themselves a Christian? As we evangelize and encounter difficult questions from those around us, we must seek to get behind their question, addressing their concerns rationally, with love, and in a trust-worthy manner.

Week four seeks to address a few common objections that our friends may have toward Christianity. This section falls under the category of apologetics. Apologetics is a branch of theology devoted to the defense of Christianity. Understanding apologetics can help you evangelize in several ways. Perhaps, as you are sharing the gospel, for example, your friend mentions having a hard time believing that the Bible is true. Week four, day one will give you tools to point to the Bible's validity and its historical credibility. Or perhaps your friend is suffering and wondering how a good God would allow such evil in the world or how Christians could justify various in-

justices throughout history. Days three and four will directly address these questions and provide biblical tools and practical tips to point to the gospel in conversation.

The following content is organized to equip you to share the gospel both in substance and method. Whether your friend's objection is primarily regarding the Bible's view of sexuality (week four, day two) or the belief that all roads lead to heaven (week four, day four), this week provides biblical answers for such questions. As you engage with others, remember to use the strategies developed in week three. Ask good questions, listen more than you speak, find common ground, and empathize with your friends. Use the content in week four to gently and lovingly transition to gospel conversation, sharing the hope that you have in Christ.

*"He is inviting us
to know Him."*

Why Do You Trust the Bible?

READ 2 TIMOTHY 3:16-17, 2 PETER 1:20-21,
HEBREWS 4:12

*"Resolution One: I will live for God.
Resolution Two: If no one else does, I still will."*

JONATHAN EDWARDS

As you share the gospel, your friend may have an objection to Christianity due to the validity of its message. Christians trust in a book that was written thousands of years ago. How could we possibly know it is true and that it has not been changed over the years? Moreover, for them the Bible feels like an outdated book that is difficult to understand and even harder to believe. It feels locked in a time and culture that is not our own, irrelevant for the problems of today. Many also suffer from what C.S. Lewis called, "chronological snobbery." We think we are more advanced than those before us, and use our own culture to judge Biblical values, rather than letting the Bible speak on its own terms. As straight-forward as this sounds, it bears repeating: just because we do not agree with a truth claim, does not mean the truth claim is wrong or illegitimate. As you discuss the authenticity and historicity of the Bible with someone, challenge your friend to read it and come to a personal conclusion.

WHAT IS THE BIBLE?

The Bible consists of 66 books. As Christians, we believe that the words of the Bible are true and are God's very words revealed to us. It is divided up into the Old Testament, which includes 39 books before Christ, and the New Testament consisting of 27 books written by the apostles and disciples of Jesus after His life, death, and resurrection.

The Bible claims to be God's Word, sufficient for all we need for life and godliness. But how do we know the Bible is not just another good book?

1. UNITY

The Bible is a unified story without contradiction. Although it was compiled over 1500 years ago, and was written by more than forty authors from vastly different backgrounds, the Bible is one big story and is completely consistent.

How were the books chosen? Movies like *The Da Vinci Code* can spark ideas of new, lost New Testament books that were hidden out of a conspiracy to hide scandalous truth. This is not true. During the Council of Hippo and the Council of Carthage, the Bible was canonized, meaning that the holy, inspired books of the Bible were affirmed. Scholars ensured that these books were affirmed by the local church, reflected evidence of the Holy Spirit, and were consistent with the rest of Scripture. In modern, non-spiritual terms, this is like editors at a publishing house ensuring that books are authentic and factual. The canon is now closed, which means that no additional books can be added or taken away from it.

2. PROPHETIC ACCURACY

The Bible contains hundreds of prophecies that have all been accurate and verified by non-religious sources. Unlike the prophecies in other religious books, these prophecies are detailed and 100% true. According to the Blue Letter Bible, there are over 270 prophecies regarding Jesus alone, including where Jesus would be born, His lineage, how He would die, and things He would say. In Peter Stoner's book, *Science Speaks*, we learn that the likelihood of even sixteen of these happening is one in 10^{45}. For perspective, there are an estimated 10^{82} atoms in the observable universe. What is more, Jesus is the fulfillment of all of these prophecies. The book, *Why Trust the Bible*, by Greg Gilbert is a great resource for more information on this topic.

3. HISTORICAL CONFIDENCE

Another affirmation to the Bible's trustworthiness is the truthfulness of its historical claims. The Bible is the best documented book from the ancient world, and its historical claims have been verified as true by historians such as Phillip Myers or the Greek historian, Arrian.

4. INDESTRUCTIBILITY

The Bible has suffered more attacks than any other book in history. From modern atheists to ancient emperors, it has been dissected and attacked by people for thousands of years. And still, it remains. It is just as relevant and true today as when it was written. Whether or not one agrees with Christianity, one must admit—something happened two thousand years ago that was so drastic that it radically affects the lives of many people today.

5. LIFE-CHANGING POWER

As Christians, we also believe the Bible because we have seen its power to change lives. The Bible has encouraged addicts to quit, restored marriages, and prompted forgiveness for the deepest of pains. It is alive and transforms us.

———

The Bible is the most popular book of all time, printed more than any other work in human history. It is just as relevant and true today as when it was written. It is not secret knowledge for a select few as some religions claim of their religious books. Its message is open and available for all to repent of their sins and believe in the risen Christ.

As we address our friend's rational concerns, we also acknowledge that there is an element of faith in trusting the words of the Bible. When the Bible expresses God's character and His love for His people, it is received by faith; just as we, in faith, choose whether to trust a friend when they say "I love you." Through the Bible, God has revealed Himself to us, and we have everything we need for life and godliness. He is inviting us to know Him, and we can confidently know Him by reading His Word, the Bible.

daily QUESTIONS

Read Matthew 23:33-35, Luke 24:44, and Luke 11:45-51. How do Jesus's words affirm Old Testament teachings?

What does 2 Timothy 3:16-17 teach you about the purpose of the Bible for the Christian today?

If we are going to defend the Bible, we should value it and know what it says. Do you have a Bible reading plan? If not, make a realistic plan to read the Bible every day this week.

"Through the Bible,
God has revealed
Himself to us, and
we have everything
we need for life
and godliness."

Tips for Sharing the Gospel with Family

• Pray with and for your family.

• Read the Bible with your children, and have conversations about what you just read.

• Children are good observers. Let your kids see how your faith impacts your everyday life. Ask them questions about their lives, and be a good listener.

• Do not assume that your kids understand the gospel because they have been in church or gone to Sunday school. Use Bible storying and other kid-friendly resources to share the truth of the gospel.

• Invite extended family into your normal rhythms, such as family worship or praying before meals. Use holidays such as Christmas and Easter to create family traditions in which you can naturally share the gospel.

• When you experience hardship, humbly share the reason you can have joy despite difficult seasons.

• Sharing the gospel with family is a long game. Do not be harsh or abrasive, but look for lingering conversations where you can share the gospel. Be kind and patient, and let your life reflect the hope and purity of the gospel.

• Be ready to share the hope in each season.

"Through the gospel, there is no fear of 'missing out.'"

126

What About Sexuality?

READ 1 CORINTHIANS 6:9-20, 1 TIMOTHY 1:15

"Missionaries are very human folks, simply a bunch of nobodies trying to exalt Somebody."

JIM ELLIOT

One of the most frequently debated topics today revolves around sexuality. Years ago, the cultural expectation was for marriage to be between a man and a woman. During this time, the narrative of society was much more apt to exclude any exceptions to this rule. As a result, the LGBTQ+ community was a source of confusion for many Christians and often received hateful and hurtful responses from the church. Today, societal norms have changed. With the legalization of same-sex marriage and the promotion of gender fluidity, same-sex attraction is much more widely accepted. To claim that living a gay lifestyle is a sin has become laughable and detestable to many, including some Christians.

As we share the gospel, it is important to keep in mind that many men and women have abandoned the faith because of the Bible's position on sexuality. While discussing sexuality, we must remember our principles of sharing the gospel—praying, observing, entering into the world of another, asking good questions, and loving the other person well. We must be loving and kind, holding to the truth and defending biblical doctrine while listening to stories about past hurts with gentleness and grace.

While discussing sexuality, we also aim to discover any underlying, fundamental objections to this topic. Do they have a family member who is gay? Have they experienced same-sex attraction? Do they have church baggage because of hurtful experiences or conversations in their past? Or are they mainly concerned with the idea of acceptance—that people should be free to make their own decisions and love whomever they want without judgment? For many people, conversations about sexuality are rooted in themes of autonomy and authenticity. As they engage with the Bible, they conclude that if this Holy God will not accept them for who they are, they would rather not follow Him. Their ultimate aim is to find fulfillment by being their true, authentic selves. They would rather live authentically than in the way that a religious institution defines as "good." Or, they might even change the words of Scripture to say that marriage between a man and a woman was a cultural norm in biblical times, not a religious command. Yet, our sexuality was never meant to be our identity, and choosing not to act on sexual desires does not mean that we are not being true to ourselves. Our true identity is found in Christ alone.

As much as possible, try to redirect the conversation to the gospel as the primary topic of conversation. Though someone may struggle with sexual desires that fall outside of God's design for our lives, the goal is not for the person to become straight or to first convert their view on homosexuality. It is our main desire that sharing the gospel with someone will lead them to their Creator, the One who made heaven and earth.

COMMON GROUND

While engaging on the topic of sexuality, we seek to find common ground. For example, we can agree with our friends that every human wants to be loved and free. We want to be known by someone, chosen by them as the most important person in the world. And we want to be free to pursue our passions. No one likes to be restricted in pursuing their desire, and we all have the innate desire to be emotionally, physically, and spiritually fulfilled. This is common ground for us both.

THE PROBLEM

(Warning: this section may trigger someone with a history of abuse or adultery.)

But what if there are no boundaries within sexual relationships? And are all sexual rules wrong? Let us remove the topic of homosexuality for a minute and examine other sexual boundaries. For example, what if your husband finds another woman attractive? Should he be free to pursue her? Or what if he wants to open your house up to a new woman (or man or child) every night? On some level, we can all agree that sexual rules are important. We can agree that if an older man finds your five-year-old daughter sexually attractive, he should not be free to act on that passion, even if she seems willing. Rules are in place to protect us and provide safety within relationships. Similarly, biblical rules on sexuality are intended for our protection.

COMMON OBJECTIONS TO BOUNDARIES OF SEXUALITY

Even if some agree with the above logic, they may still have some objections to biblical boundaries on homosexuality. Below we will discuss some common objections to the boundary, along with the biblical reasoning for such boundaries.

Why would the Bible call homosexuality wrong when it is not hurting anyone? Should not two consenting adults be free to love one another? Is the Bible not outdated on this topic anyway?

When God made rules for mankind, He did not make laws to be mean or restrictive like an evil father trying to steal gifts from his children. Rather, He designed rules that are for our good, like a fence that protects your children from running out into a busy street. When God made man and woman, He created rules for marriage and sexuality. He planned for man and woman to leave their father and mother and become one flesh (Genesis 2:24). He designed that marriage would serve as a reflection of Christ's love for the church (Ephesians 5:31-32). This one-flesh relationship is an exclusive love between a husband and wife. This marriage relationship is called to be for a man and woman, and the Bible clearly explains that it is a sin to join together sexually with someone from the same gender (Romans 1:26-27).

Some people interpret these verses to say that they were culturally relevant but are now outdated. In doing so, they misread the Bible's clarity on this subject. Same-sex attraction existed in Paul's day. In fact, Plato's *Symposium* details the the myth about Zeus, a Greek god, creating heterosexual and homosexual humans. So, we know that some ancients accepted homosexual practices because it is built into their creation myths. Paul is not saying that homosexuality is the worst of all sins, but he does call it a sin. (For more on this, read 1 Timothy 1:9-10, 1 Corinthians 6:9, Romans 1:26-27.)

What about those who identify as LGBTQ+? Surely these desires come from God, and He would want them to be fulfilled, right?

When Adam and Eve rebelled against God in the Garden of Eden, brokenness was introduced into every area of our lives, including our sexuality. Every single person is broken and struggles in sin. At one point or another, most Christians have desired sexual intimacy with someone other than their spouse, whether male or female. And how many Christian men and women are addicted to porn and instant gratification, rather than choosing abstinence or sexually devoting themselves to their spouses? Being a Christian does not exempt us from sexual sin, and holiness does not preclude temptations of many kinds. We are all broken in this area—desiring sexual satisfaction in unhealthy and unholy ways.

That said, marriage and sexual satisfaction were never meant to fulfill us. As Rebecca McLaughlin explains in *Confronting Christianity*, marriage is not the pinnacle of love but a different form of love governed by boundaries. While the call to follow God may be a call to surrender desires for a season, it is a call to longing, not loneliness. Every unfulfilled desire in this life is meant to point to something greater and reminds us that this world is not our home. As C.S. Lewis says, "If we find ourselves with a desire that nothing in this world can satisfy, the most probable explanation is that we were made for another world." Through the gospel, there is no fear of "missing out." Saying "no" to sexual desires does not seem like an unspeakable request because we know that something better is coming. Furthermore, through the church, God puts the lonely into families. He gives us brothers and sisters, mothers and fathers, through men and women in the church. Christian friendships are not consolation prizes, either. Indeed, we are called by God to have deeper same-sex friendships than most Christians ever attain (John 15:13, 1 Samuel 18).

We all desire for God to accept us as we are, but God offers us something even better. He sees us wholly, loves us fully, and covers our sin through His Son. Through Christ, we are fully known and loved. He calls us near in our sin and brokenness, and He does not leave us in this brokenness. If we want this kind of relationship, true freedom, and love, we must turn from our ways and trust in Christ's life, death, and resurrection. When we surrender everything, even our sexual desires to the Lord, He offers us true satisfaction—peace, wholeness, and love. He gives us purpose and calls us His friends.

Marriage and human love is not the ultimate gift. In heaven, there will not be marriage (Matthew 22:30), but instead, we will finally be united with our true love, the One who satisfies us completely. When we see God face to face, it will be better than we can ever imagine. Christ offers us something even greater than momentary sexual fulfillment; He offers us eternal peace.

WHEN WE SURRENDER EVERYTHING, EVEN OUR SEXUAL DESIRES TO THE LORD, HE OFFERS US TRUE SATISFACTION—PEACE, WHOLENESS, AND LOVE.

Read 1 Timothy 1:9-10, 1 Corinthians 6:9, and Romans 1:26-27.
What does the Bible say about sexuality?

_____

_____

_____

_____

_____

_____

What are some other ways that we can be sexually sinful? Is there any superiority to these struggles?

_____

_____

_____

_____

_____

_____

Consider 1 Corinthians 6:9-11. How has our identity been changed through Christ?

_____

_____

_____

_____

_____

_____

_____

_____

"We all desire for God to accept us as we are, but God offers us something even better."

Tips for Sharing the Gospel with Friends

- Love your friends well. Talk about topics that matter to them. Engage in intentional, meaningful conversations about beauty, work, music, and culture. Look for bridges to share how the gospel informs your view on these topics.

- Ask how you can be praying for them. Follow up on the issues for which they have asked for prayer.

- If you have talked about spiritual things, offer to read the Bible together so that they can determine who Jesus is for themselves. The book of Mark can be a good place to start because it is fast-paced and the shortest of the gospels. Read a chapter together, and ask questions such as:

    -*What did you think about this reading?*

    -*What did you learn about God?*

    -*What did you learn about man?*

    -*What does it teach you about how God relates with man?*

    -*Is there anything you think you should do based on today's reading?*

- Use hospitality to invite others into your home. Dessert is often not as scary of a commitment as dinner, so invite someone to coffee or dessert at your home.

- Frequent the same establishments to build relationships with baristas, clerks, and other workers.

- As you spend time with someone, inevitably, you will find something that is broken. Be ready to share how God is the fulfillment of these desires. For example, for the one struggling with loneliness, we can share about how God is our closest companion. Or, for one struggling with overeating, how God is the craving our hearts ultimately desire.

- Look for bridges to the gospel through conversations about work, weekend plans, current events, or worldview topics such as beauty or creativity.

- Ask lots of questions. Be friendly, and let them talk longer than you do. Be kind and servant-hearted.

"*The gospel is what brings hope for the broken-hearted.*"

Why is There Suffering?

READ 2 CORINTHIANS 1:1-11

*"Jesus promised his disciples three things: they would be completely
fearless, absurdly happy, and in constant trouble."*

WILLIAM BARCLAY

Cancer. Death. Abuse. Exhaustion. Pandemic. Abandonment. False Accusations. If we live long enough, we will discover that suffering and hardship affect us all. Though we are believers, precious and loved by God, we are not exempt from suffering. Instead, when we are in Christ, we wrestle, struggle and cry out to the Lord through our sufferings. Despite uncertainty, anguish, and internal pain, we have the assurance that somehow, mysteriously, God will use all things for His glory and our good (Romans 8:28). But for those who are not yet believers, the question of suffering can be a major obstacle to faith. If there is a good and powerful God, how could He allow such bad things to happen?

Usually, when someone asks about suffering as an objection to Christianity it is because they have deep pain in their lives. Maybe they have experienced abuse, suffering, or the loss of a loved one. The idea of a loving, powerful God seems hurtful, even impossible. In these moments, pray for sensitivity, and be a good listener. This is not the time to enter into a debate, but rather to open your heart to them. As we see with Job's friends, it is better to listen to someone and cry with them in their pain than debate them on the doctrine of suffering (Job 4-23). The role of a friend is to love well in word and deed and not necessarily give easy answers for their pain.

While determining which route you should take in conversation, start with the question, "Why do you ask?" as this objection is usually a personal one. If you determine that the person you are talking to has primarily an ethical objection to suffering and the existence of God, here are a few tools to engage in conversation.

WHAT IS SUFFERING?

Suffering is the deep ache that comes from living in a fallen world. This may manifest itself in grief, sorrow, loss, or pain. It can be internal, such as depression, grief, or anxiety. Or it can be due to external factors, such as conflict or catastrophe. In suffering, we ache, lament and hurt, longing to rid ourselves of the deep, gnawing pain.

WHY IS THERE SUFFERING?

If we do not believe in God, other explanations for suffering are limited. Where did the world come from, and where are we going? Why are some people evil, while others just want to be left alone? Why do cancer, car accidents, or abuse affect young children? Is there any justice in the world?

As Christians, we believe that suffering is the result of sin in the world. When Adam and Eve sinned in the garden, brokenness reached into every area of our lives. While the term "sin" might feel outdated to some, we all recognize its effects, from corruption to poverty and manipulation to war. You need only to look at the news to see the brokenness in the world: conflict, disease, division, and death. Truly there is something terribly wrong with the world.

God did not make the world this way. He made the world good. He made every man, woman, and child in His image and provided for their needs (Genesis 1:27-31). God could have designed us to be thoughtless, loyal subjects. He is all-powerful and can do whatever He pleases. But instead, He created mankind and wanted to give us the opportunity to make our own decisions. He gave us free will, and we chose to disobey. God gave people good rules and laws for our own benefit, but we rebelled (Deuteronomy 1:1-4:43). He provided protection for the weak, but as humans, we despised the weak and sought to protect ourselves or our kind. As we withdrew from our Creator, we detached from the very source of goodness itself.

TRANSITION TO THE GOSPEL

In His mercy, God saw this crippling brokenness and sent a rescue mission through His Son. The escape to our suffering is not found through death, suicide, or numbing addictive behaviors. The answer is found in Christ.

In suffering, it can feel like God is far away. But through the gospel, we know that God loved us so much that He drew near. When Jesus came, He left the splendors of Heaven to live a human life, and in doing so, endured the greatest suffering of all. He was betrayed, condemned, falsely accused, and beaten. He was humiliated and murdered, hanging naked on a cross for all to see. He is not a far-off God, watching sternly from Heaven and waiting for us to mess up. He is tender and provided a way for us to be made right with Him again (Luke 1:77-78).

Why would anyone suffer this for us? When Jesus endured this ultimate suffering, He destroyed the power of sin and offered salvation for all who would believe. He took on our sins and paid the penalty that we deserved. And in His resurrection, He offers us new life with Him.

The gospel is what brings hope for the broken-hearted. One day, God will make everything right again. He will judge the world and bring perfect justice to mankind. He will wipe away every tear, and there will be no more pain or sorrow for those who trust Him (Revelation 21:4). For those who are in Christ, He promises to use even the worst suffering for our good. Christ, known as the Suffering Servant, has mercy on us. He prays for us, sustains us, and helps us when we are weak. He does not pull away from us because of our weakness, as if we somehow tarnish His perfect holiness. Rather, He bends near, drawing us close and binding our wounds. He heals, equips, strengthens, and upholds (Psalm 147:3, Ephesians 2:13, Ephesians 6:10).

If there is no God, then the justice we see on Earth is all that there is. But as Christians, we believe that God is holy and will right every wrong and heal every hurt. In light of who He is, we gladly repent of our sins and follow this loving God. He sees all of the injustices and sorrows we face, and one day He will make all things right.

daily QUESTIONS

Read 1 Peter 2:21-25 and 1 Peter 3:17-22. How did Christ enter into our sufferings?

Read Romans 8:28-30. What is the hope of suffering for the Christian?

Think of someone in your life who is hurting. Pray for sensitivity and the ability to enter into their pain. Brainstorm ways that you can tangibly love them this week.

"He bends near, drawing us close and binding our wounds. He heals, equips, strengthens, and upholds."

Tips for Sharing the Gospel with Strangers

From time to time, you may find yourself engaged with a stranger in conversation as you sit on the subway or in the parking lot at the grocery store. As conversation flows, you see that you are easily able to enter into a discussion of worldview and glimpse an opening to share the gospel. Here are a few tips to remember:

- Ask questions, and look for a bridge to spiritual conversation.

- Be prepared with a three-minute or less presentation of the gospel. Know your main points, and do not get side-tracked with other secondary issues.

- If given the chance, share your testimony.

- Ask how you can be praying for them.

- It may be a good idea to leave a gospel booklet or something to read over if you cannot finish the conversation. If you feel comfortable doing so, you can also leave your phone number for a follow-up conversation.

- Go with another brother or sister in your church to follow up, if possible.

"Seek to find common ground in conversation."

Are Not All Religions the Same?

"The great commission is not an option to be considered;
it is a command to be obeyed."

ATTRIBUTED TO HUDSON TAYLOR

Is there only one right religion? Does absolute truth exist? How do we know what is true? And who are you to impose your religion on someone else? These are questions that frequently underlie many evangelistic conversations. Christians who claim to know "the truth" are often perceived as arrogant and close-minded. Society no longer believes in absolute truth. Rather, many believe in a post-modern world where each person is entitled to their own truth. Many believe that God is like a spiritual force, such as karma. He is amorphous, distant, and vague. He does not care who comes to Him but sees our good intentions and freely welcomes all.

COMMON GROUND

As we share the gospel, if the question of religious truth arises, we should seek to find common ground in conversation. We can identify common longings within this question, such as the desire to be accepted. We all want there to be peace in the world and for there to be respect among people of different religions. The idea that "some are in, and others are out" is a difficult concept. We want everyone to be free, loved, good, and accepted.

THE PROBLEM

Around the world, many people view religion as the ancient folk tale from India of the blind men and the elephant. According to the old Indian proverb, several blind men were introduced to an elephant for the first time. They each touched the elephant and used their limited experience to describe what the animal was like. One man touched the trunk and described the elephant as a thick snake. Another man touched its ear and described it as a fan. One man touched its leg and described the elephant like a tree trunk; while another touched its tail, describing it as a rope. As one man felt the elephant's side, he called it a wall. Finally, the last man touched the elephant's tusk, describing it as hard and smooth, like a spear. This story expresses the underlying belief in multiple truths. Each man had a limited perspective and could not understand the whole shape of the elephant.

The problem with this analogy is that it is limited. As Sam Chan illustrates in his book *Evangelism in a Skeptical World*, the elephant has a real shape, but the men do not know what it is. But what if the elephant could talk? What if the elephant said, "I am not a rope, or a tree trunk, or a spear. I am an elephant. This is what I am like." If the elephant were able to reveal Himself to the men through its words, they would be able to know what he is like. Better still, what if the elephant had the power to open the eyes of the blind so that they could see? As Christians, we believe that God has spoken to us through His Word, the Bible. He has revealed Himself to us and opened our eyes to see the way to eternal life through Jesus.

The concept of a vague God may appeal to many people. After all, a vague God is better than an angry one, is He not? And is inclusivity not better than exclusivity? When Jesus came, however, He was not soft or vague. He spoke a radical message and claimed to be God. He told His followers that there is only one way to be saved. And that one way is through belief in Him. His message was not neutral, hazy, or amorphous. As we examine the radical claims that Jesus made about Himself, we must make conclusions about who we think He is. There is no room for naive inclusivity with Jesus's claims.

TRANSITIONING TO THE GOSPEL

To use another popular analogy, some believe that the kingdom of heaven is like a mountain. The goal is to get to the top of the mountain to be with God, but it does not matter how this is achieved. Some choose Hinduism, others Buddhism, but they each strive to climb according to their own methods. The problem with this analogy, as stated by David Platt in *Radical*, however, is that no person can get to the top of the mountain on their own. The terrain is too difficult, the mountain too steep. All who have tried perish. We are helpless on our own and cannot get to God. We need a God who will come down to us, and that is what Jesus did.

While all other religions focus on what we need to do, be, or become, the message of the gospel is about what Jesus has already done. He is the God who descended down the mountain to bring us to the Father. He came down from heaven, lived a perfect life, and died the death that we deserve. He defeated sin and came alive from the grave. And He will one day return to rule over Earth. Those who trust in Him will be brought into His Kingdom where we will live and reign with Him. God has provided a way for all to come to Him by believing in Jesus.

We believe that God is many things—good, perfect, loving, and just. Yet, while He is many things, He is not vague. He has revealed Himself to us through the Bible and given us all that we need for life and godliness. He is gracious and patient, not wanting any to perish but all to come to repentance. There is only one way to be right with God, through His Son, who paid the penalty that we deserve and offers us a new life.

daily QUESTIONS

Read Romans 1:19-21. How has humankind responded to God's revelation of Himself?

How are we saved? Read Acts 16:31.

Read John 1:1, 14. How did the Father reveal Himself to us?

"While all others religions
focus on what we need
to do, be, or become,
the message of the
gospel is about what
Jesus has already done."

Accountability Questions

If you want to grow in evangelism, two factors are extremely important: accountability and celebration. Ask a friend to keep you accountable by asking the following questions, and praise God when given the opportunity to share the gospel!

Have you shared your faith with someone this week?

If not, what kept you from sharing your faith this week?

What action steps do you need to take to grow in your ability to evangelize?

"*He destroyed the penalty of sin for all who would believe.*"

Doesn't Christianity Promote Injustice?

READ LUKE 4:18-21, LUKE 10:27-37, MATTHEW 5:44

*"The biggest hindrance to the missionary task is self.
Self that refuses to die. Self that refuses to sacrifice.
Self that refuses to give. Self that refuses to go."*

THOMAS HALE, MISSIONARY TO NEPAL

At times, a friend may have walls up against Christianity because of systemic injustices of Christians in the past. Perhaps this is due to racism, the Crusades, or their interpretation of the Bible's view of women. As we engage with this question, we must seek first to find common ground. We agree that injustice is wrong. Not everyone who claims to be a Christian is truly a Christian (Matthew 7:21-23), and even real Christians have blindspots. Slavery is abhorrent, and abuse is unacceptable. Once we understand that men and women throughout history have distorted the Bible and used its words to justify their horrific actions, we can transition to and understand the hope found in the gospel.

WHY HAVE CHRISTIANS DONE _____ INJUSTICE?

Whether regarding slavery, the Crusades, or sexism, it is wrong for someone to use Christianity to justify their sinful actions. It is horrible and condemned by God. God does not approve of these injustices, and He did not want the world to be this way. Although God created a good world, humankind rebelled against God, and sin was introduced into the world. Sin brought evil and division to every area of human life, including race and gender.

Deep down, we are all sinners and could commit even the worst of crimes if put in the wrong situation at the wrong time. It is not socially beneficial for one living in middle-class America to kill or steal, but if one is hungry or under attack in a poverty-stricken third-world country, the sin within one could lead to horrific results apart from the grace of God. We see this in every human heart, and sadly, every major religion holds an ugly history of violence, including Christianity, Islam, and Buddhism.

TRANSITIONING TO THE GOSPEL

The truth of the gospel is that Jesus came for the broken, the vulnerable, the weak, and the poor. He came to give them life and bring restoration to the brokenness of this world. He spoke with, loved, and empowered those from different backgrounds, ethnicities, and races. He was the only one who ever lived a perfect life, and when He died on the cross, He destroyed the penalty of sin for all who would believe. Far from not caring about injustice and suffering, Jesus entered into our suffering. He did this so that one day, we will not have to suffer any longer. He is the answer to the world's problems, and one day He will judge the world to make all things right. This is the Christian's hope.

It is important to note that even though you may have never committed a heinous crime, you too have done bad things. You may have been socially unjust due to unconscious biases toward those created in His image. Or you may struggle with lying, cheating, or anger. Either way, all have rebelled against the Holy God. Thanks be to God. He had mercy on you and saved you. And He promises that whoever believes in Him will not only be set free from the power of sin today but live with Him in the life to come. You will live in a land with no suffering, pain, or trial. He is the almighty judge and will not allow the guilty to

go unpunished. One day He will make all things whole again and right every wrong.

TWO COMMON OBJECTIONS TO CHRISTIANITY

Many object to Christianity because they believe it is racist and suppresses women. However, these assumptions are often based on the actions of people who claim to be Christians but do not follow God's Word concerning the treatment of others. Below are two common objections to Christianity, along with the biblical response to those objections.

Christianity is Racist

Christianity, in its essence, is anti-racist. It is inclusive of people from every background, income, and gender. It destroys the facade of power and instead calls us to be servants of one another out of reverence for Christ. The New Testament message was not one of dominance and power but humility and weakness. There is no place for superiority or exploitation within the church. But because of sin, people band together against those who are unlike them with hatred and racism. Slavery and the exploitation of other humans are results of the fall, and God does not approve of these injustices. Instead, He will judge every human sin, including the sin of racism.

Today, there can often be a suspicion toward Christianity because of abuse and injustice committed by those who bear the name of "Christian." Pictures of a white Jesus pervade Sunday School rooms, and Bible verses are wrongly interpreted and used to justify racist behaviors. Jesus has harsh words toward those who abuse others while claiming to know Him (Matthew 7:7-12, 21-23). Christianity did not start in the West, nor is it only for white Americans. Jesus was not Western nor is Christianity. Today, most of the world's Christians are statistically not white, and indeed many effective missionary efforts are currently happening through nationals reaching their own people groups.

Every human being is made in God's image and of infinite worth to Him. The message of the gospel is not one of earthly power or domination but humility and weakness. Jesus left His perfect home in heaven to live on this dirty earth and experience excruciating pain. He came for the poor, the hurting, and the abused. He became a slave so that we might be set free from our bondage to sin (Philippians 2:7). And He came to offer freedom and give life for all who would repent of their sins and follow Him.

Christianity Makes Women Inferior to Men

When God made Eve, He made her as Adam's helper. This can seem offensive until we realize that the word "helper" was also used to refer to God (Exodus 18:4, Deuteronomy 33:26, 29, Psalm 20:2, 33:20, 118:7, Hosea 13:9). It is not a word of weakness, just as submission is not a sign of inferiority. The problem is that many men have abused their positions of authority using dominance and threats. This is wrong and an injustice before God and mankind.

TRANSITIONING TO THE GOSPEL

When Jesus came, He flipped societal norms on their head. He commanded those who are strong to serve the weak and said the greatest among you must be your servant (Matthew 20:26-28). In the Bible, Jesus gave value to women. He spoke to those who were not considered socially acceptable (Luke 7:36-50, Luke 13:16-17) and told husbands to love their wives as Christ loved the Church (Ephesians 5:25). And how did He love the Church? By sacrificing Himself and dying for the Church so that we could be saved. Submission in the Bible does not make someone less valuable. Indeed, Jesus Himself submitted to God the Father. He valued and gave worth to women. And for all who believe in Him, He calls His children and lavishes His love on them, regardless of gender.

———

Notice that in these discussions, we have included the four points of the gospel: creation, fall, redemption, restoration. We discuss God, the problem (sin), and the solution (Christ). God did not want or approve of the exploitation of others, and sin has pervaded all aspects of life. As Christians, we must examine our own lives and search out even latent, unconscious sin. We all come needy to the Father, and the solution is found in Christ. After this discussion, we can ask for a response from our listeners as we engage with their perspectives and acknowledge their hurts.

WHEN JESUS CAME, HE FLIPPED SOCIETAL NORMS ON THEIR HEAD.

daily QUESTIONS

What does Romans 1:20-32 reveal about the sinfulness of man?

_____

_____

_____

_____

_____

_____

Read Galatians 3:27-28 and Philemon 1:15-16. How does the message of the gospel change one's social standing?

_____

_____

_____

_____

_____

Read Ephesians 5:22-33. How does submission within marriage reflect the gospel?

_____

_____

_____

_____

_____

_____

_____

"The truth of the gospel
is that Jesus came
for the broken, the
vulnerable, the weak,
and the poor."

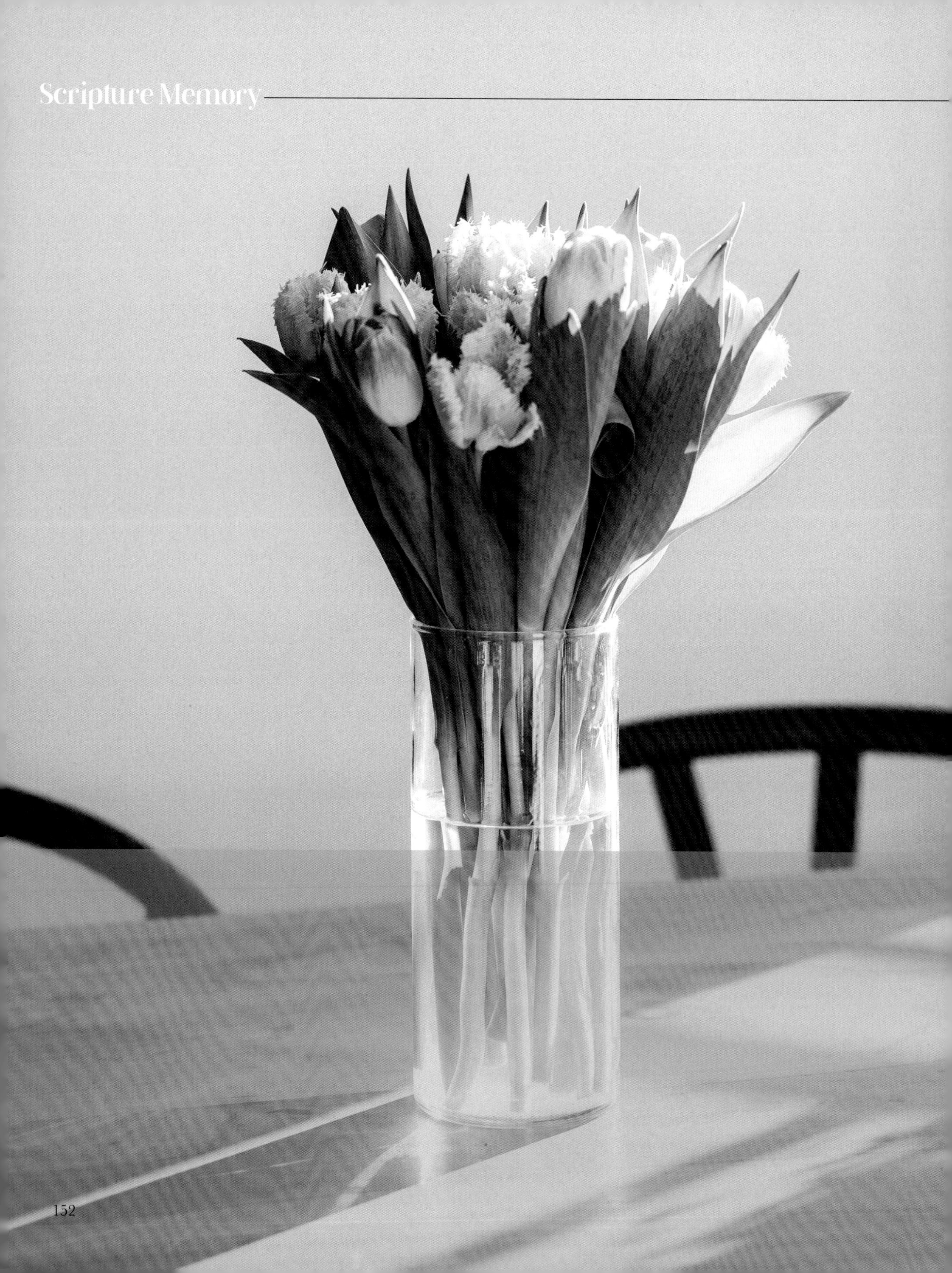

For I am not ashamed
of the gospel, because it
is the power of God for
salvation to everyone who
believes, first to the Jew,
and also to the Greek.

ROMANS 1:16

weekly REFLECTION

Review all Scripture passages from the week.

Summarize the main points from this week's Scripture readings.

_____   _____
_____   _____
_____   _____
_____   _____
_____   _____
_____   _____
_____   _____
_____   _____
_____   _____
_____   _____

What did you observe from this week's passages about God and His character?

_____
_____
_____
_____
_____
_____

What do this week's passages reveal about the condition of mankind and yourself?

_____
_____
_____
_____
_____

How do these passages point to the gospel?

How should you respond to these Scriptures? What specific action steps
can you take this week to apply them in your life?

Write a prayer in response to your study of God's Word. Adore God for who He is,
confess sins He revealed in your own life, ask Him to empower you to walk in obedience,
and pray for anyone who comes to mind as you study.

Sharing by Themes

Week five offers sample gospel presentations for friends who are in various life stages. Whether your friend is overwhelmed by shame or sees no need for God, this week's study seeks to equip you with the tools and language to share the gospel with them. Ideally, each gospel presentation will be shared, not as a monologue presented to your friends but rather as a discussion with your friends. Similarly, these prompts are not meant to be read out loud verbatim to your non-believing friends. Rather, they serve as simple models for how to share the gospel contextually, given your friend's experience.

As you share, remember to consider the information from weeks one through four. Pray, be kind, listen well, and ask good questions. Pray for opportunities to share the gospel and that God would open the hearts of your friends, neighbors, and family members.

66

Pray, be kind, listen well, and ask good questions.

"*Jesus entered into our suffering.*"

For the One Who is Suffering

|

READ PSALM 46, ACTS 13:47

"If I had not felt certain that every additional trial was ordered by infinite love and mercy, I could not have survived my accumulated suffering."

ADONIRAM JUDSON

As described in week four, the problem of suffering can be a stumbling block for many. They simply cannot believe that a good God would allow evil in the world.

At the same time, suffering can also catalyze reflection, searching, and openness. When the world feels dark, and pain pierces deeply, we are often forced to reconsider our previous assumptions and priorities. We may come to realizations such as, "I was living for my job, giving everything to it. But is success really what matters in the end?" or "My main goal in life was to be wealthy and comfortable, but then this health diagnosis came. Now I am afraid and weak. I am not comfortable, and I am miserable inside. What is the use of having all this money if I cannot even enjoy it?"

When the foundations of our friends and family crumble, as often happens during suffering, we have an opportunity to share the gospel in love. As much as possible, try to enter into your friend's pain by being compassionate. Be slow to speak and quick to listen. Grieve with your friend, rather than offer trite solutions for the pain. Remember to speak kindly, listen well, and engage with grace. Hurt people often hurt people, so if your friend responds harshly in the midst of suffering, be gracious and quick to forgive. Let your love for your friend flow not only through your tone of voice but also through your actions. Bring that person a meal, watch their kids so they can sleep, or buy their groceries. Pray for your friend, and lovingly point them in word and deed (Romans 15:18) to the hope found in Jesus.

A GOSPEL PRESENTATION FOR THE ONE WHO IS SUFFERING

As you identify suffering or brokenness in life, you can use this topic to transition to the gospel. As you grieve with your friend, supporting and loving them well, you may share something like:

I am so sorry for your pain. It grieves me that life is like this and that you suffered this loss. I hate that there is so much brokenness in the world. It is everywhere, and sometimes it feels like we cannot escape it. From miscarriages to murder and death to deceit, we can all see that this world is not as it should be. Many people try to cope with this brokenness by escaping or distracting themselves. Maybe they plunge themselves into work, relationships, or exercise. Or maybe they run from their problems to drugs, sex, or binge eating. But in the end, these behaviors always leave us feeling emptier than when we began. They drive us right back into our suffering.

When God made the world, He did not make it this way. God is the source of all love, joy, and goodness. He made us to walk with Him and talk with Him, experiencing perfect peace and joy. There was no death, decay, or disease. There was no maliciousness or abuse of power. The problem is that mankind rebelled against God, thinking that life would be better on their own. They went against God's commands, and when they did this, death and sin were introduced into the world.

Thankfully, God did not leave us there, stuck in our brokenness and shame. He made a way for us to be restored to God by sending His own Son, Jesus. Fully God and fully man, Jesus entered into our suffering. He came close, dirtied His feet, and ate with prostitutes and thieves. Not only this, but Jesus suffered the worst suffering any person will ever experience. He was betrayed by His closest friends. He was hungry, beaten, mocked, and despised. He was tortured and murdered.

Though He was the perfect one, full of goodness and love, Jesus died a criminal's death on a cross. Even while He was completely innocent, He willingly died for our sins. He took on the weight of all of the bad things His children did and paid for them on the cross through His perfect sacrifice. But not only this, He came to life again! He appeared to His followers and more than 500 people, and He is now at the right hand of God, praying for and helping all those who trust in Him.

When we repent of our sins and put our faith in Jesus, He promises to adopt us as His children. He cleanses our guilt and shame. He covers us, protects us, and fights for us. Our God is not far off, sitting in His ivory castle in heaven, distant from the world. Instead, He is here, in your suffering, and He will one day return to make all things right.

Have you ever heard this before? What are your thoughts? What is keeping you from trusting Him today?

FINAL THOUGHTS

As you share the gospel, remember that salvation comes from the Lord. It is possible that the Spirit is already at work within someone's life such that they are ready to receive the gospel immediately upon hearing it. An example of this is the Ethiopian eunuch in Acts 8. As Philip was on the road from Jerusalem to Gaza, he encountered a man who was sitting in a chariot and reading the book of Isaiah. Philip asked the man if he understood what he was reading, and he responded that he did not. When Philip shared how the passage that he was reading in Isaiah pointed to the good news of Jesus, the man believed and was immediately baptized. Or, we may be one person among many who will share the gospel. As in 1 Corinthians 3:6-9, it may be our job to plant the seed or water it, but God always gives the growth. Our job is to faithfully and lovingly share the hope of God with others. It is God's job to save. If you share the gospel with someone and that person does not believe right away, take heart. God moves on His timeline, and He has the power to save your friend or family member.

daily QUESTIONS

How has God used suffering in your life to draw you closer to Himself?

Consider 2 Corinthians 1:3-11. How does God use our suffering to help others?

Sometimes people wonder if they are suffering because they are being punished. While there are consequences to our decisions, there is also brokenness in the world that causes suffering beyond our comprehension. Read John 9:1-5 and Job 1 and reflect on some of the reasons God allows suffering.

"We all feel a deep sense that something is not right."

For the One Who is Overwhelmed by Shame

READ LUKE 8:43-48

"His authority on earth allows us to dare to go to all the nations.
His authority in heaven gives us our only hope of success.
And His presence with us leaves us no other choice."

JOHN STOTT

Shame is a common human experience. It makes us feel dirty and unclean. We struggle with underlying feelings of unworthiness, failure, and brokenness. We may feel shame because of something we have done wrong or because of something that has been done to us. But while guilt says, "I have done something wrong," shame cuts deeper. Shame says, "I am wrong. I am a bad parent. I am a failure. I am worthless. I am not enough."

While some try to distract themselves from their shame, others wallow in it. Neither of these solutions ultimately works because we cannot circumvent shame. In truth, we do all have shame before our Maker. We all have fallen short of God's perfect standard and feel the effect of our sin. Our shame cannot be avoided, and we cannot remove it. The only answer to our shame is found in Christ.

COMMON GROUND

We all have a shame problem. Because of the fall, brokenness was introduced to every aspect of our lives. We all feel a deep sense that something is not right. If someone you love is experiencing shame, there are a few things you can do. First, be patient, and lovingly remind them of your care for them. Second, share about your shame and how you found hope in Christ. Finally, share how the gospel helped you overcome your shame and how the loving protection of God set you free.

A GOSPEL PRESENTATION FOR THE ONE EXPERIENCING SHAME

You may also have the opportunity to share a Bible story about shame with your friend. For example, you may say something like, "It seems like you are really feeling bad about yourself. I love you and am here for you. I really want you to know how much you are loved. There is actually a story I love about a woman who was feeling ashamed and found wholeness. It is a beautiful story. Can I share it with you?" Then share a story like this one from Luke 8:

> *Thousands of years ago, during the time of Jesus, there was a woman who had been bleeding for twelve years. She had seen all the doctors and taken all the medicine, but nothing helped. According to Old Testament law, anyone who was bleeding was sent outside the camp. They were considered unclean and shunned by the public. This woman, then, was viewed as dirty, not because of anything she had done but because of a physical disease. She could not touch anyone, and if she so much as bumped into someone, they were considered unclean too. Can you imagine how lonely she must have felt? How shameful, dirty, and alone?*
>
> *One day, this woman heard of a man named Jesus who was coming into town. Though she was ceremonially unclean and was required to be separate from others (Leviticus 15:19), she joined the bustling, pushing crowd to see Him. People were calling Jesus a healer, saying He had cast out demons and healed people of their diseases (Luke 7:1-17, 8:1-4). She likely wondered, against all odds—was there hope for her too? Could Jesus heal her disease? With what remained of her hope, she went out to see Jesus.*
>
> *The crowd was bustling that day, everyone pressing in to touch or even get a glimpse of Jesus. What could she do? So she reached out her hand to touch His clothes. Immediately, her bleeding stopped.*
>
> *Even though the crowds were pressing in, Jesus knew this specific woman's story. He stopped in the crowd and asked, "Who touched me?" Trembling, she came forward and revealed herself. Jesus looked at the woman and tenderly called her "Daughter." He affirmed that her faith had healed her and restored her to the community. He did not condemn the woman or shun her; He loved her. Her dirtiness did not pollute Him; He made her clean.*
>
> *That is what Jesus does. When Jesus died on the cross, He took on all of our guilt and shame and destroyed it. He does not ignore our shame or say it is not important. He covers it with His righteousness. For all who would believe in His perfect life, death,*

and resurrection, He offers a new identity. Instead of broken, despicable nobodies, He calls us whole, beloved sons and daughters. He removes our shame and replaces it with cleanness, love, and purpose.

Friend, I know that you feel unlovable and dirty. Just like Jesus made this woman clean, He is here to help you, comfort you, and take care of you. If we turn from our sins and trust in Christ, we find true and lasting peace. This woman had to take a leap of faith to reach out her hand to touch Him, risking everything to see this man who can heal. Are you willing to take this same leap of faith?

daily QUESTIONS

What are some reasons you have felt shame throughout your life? How has the gospel brought healing in those areas?

_____

_____

_____

Read Leviticus 15:19-30. How does the Old Testament describe uncleanness due to bleeding? How did Jesus change this woman's destiny?

_____

_____

_____

_____

Read Hebrews 12:2. What did Jesus do to shame on the cross?

_____

_____

_____

_____

"*There is something even better.*"

For the One Who Sees No Need for Christ

READ ROMANS 3:10-12, PSALM 14:1-3

"Sympathy is no substitute for action."

DAVID LIVINGSTONE

Sometimes our friends see no need for Christ. Life feels calm and stable. They are thriving in their careers and are happy and healthy. The future seems to be very much within their control. Admittedly, this is one of the most difficult circumstances in which to share the gospel. Only the sick need a doctor, and Christ came to save sinners, not the righteous (Mark 2:17). When someone feels broken, it can be easier for them to see their need for Christ. But when someone is proud, it is often more difficult to recognize their need for a Savior.

If this describes your friend or family member, be patient. Open the door for gospel conversations, but do not be forceful with them. Engage in deeper world-view conversations about purpose, family, and hope. Seek to be a good friend, and love your friends or family where they are. Go to their events and birthday parties. Get excited about what matters to them. As you invest in what matters to them, they will likely become curious about what matters to you.

If given the opportunity, you can also ask your friend a question like, "Do you have a faith?" As they share what they believe, do not be harsh or aggressive. Rather, express interest and ask follow-up questions. Get them to talk as much as possible. Say something like, "Wow, interesting! Tell me about that." When they reverse the question, be prepared to give an answer for what you believe.

As you seek to share the gospel with self-sufficient individuals, also think about the structure of your friend groups. Instead of having your Christian friends and your non-Christian friends as two separate groups, try to converge the two. Maybe you can invite your Christian friends to join a community soccer team together. Or perhaps you can go to the gym with people from your church. This gives you a great opportunity to evangelize together and encourage one another.

COMMON GROUND

When someone is in a happy, self-sufficient season of life, we can empathize with their happiness because we all want to live joyful lives. We want to be free from pain, healthy, and successful.

Sometimes we experience seasons of extraordinary blessing when life is calm, and everything seems to be going well. This is a blessing from God and a gift to be enjoyed!

TRANSITION TO THE GOSPEL

It is not that the blessings of health or prosperity are bad, but there is something even better. As C.S. Lewis says, "It would seem that Our Lord finds our desires not too strong, but too weak. We are half-hearted creatures, fooling about with drink and sex and ambition when infinite joy is offered us, like an ignorant child who wants to go on making mud pies in a slum because he cannot imagine what is meant by the offer of a holiday at the sea. We are far too easily pleased." The happiness we experience in a good meal or a fulfilling conversation are but a glimpse of the overwhelming joy available to those who trust in Christ.

"BUT I AM NOT THAT BAD"

Sometimes our friends will say that religion is for the weak or that they are a good person who does not need a Savior. If they express this belief, try to emphasize God's holiness and the gravity of even a "small" sin. For example, you may say something like:

Yes, you are right. Some people have committed heinous crimes, and I see that you try to be a good person. You love your family, you are honest at work, and you are kind to others. And yet, even when life is going well, I know that I still have days when I respond harshly toward my co-worker or get angry at my spouse. I still fall short, even when life is good. This is because Jesus raised the standard past the "most extreme" sins like murder and adultery, and instead, He looks to the heart. Jesus said that if we have ever been angry in our hearts against a brother, it is the same as if we have murdered them (Matthew 5:21-23). He said that if we have looked at another man or woman lustfully, it is the same as if we have had an affair with them (Matthew 5:27-28). This is because the heart of both of these sins is the same: hate and lust. Even if we have not murdered, cheated, or stolen from the IRS, we have all fallen short of God's perfect standard.

While this may seem extreme, consider this comparison: even a little sin pollutes the heart in the same that a little bit of dirt pollutes clean water. As a crude example, if a small amount of feces dropped into your large glass of water, is the water still clean? Would you still drink it? While the excrement piece might seem small compared to the amount of water, a little bit dirties the whole bottle. In the same way, before a perfect God, we are unclean, and even a little sin makes all of us dirty, worthy of judgment.

The only hope for our sins is found in Jesus, who lived a perfect life, died on a cross for our sins, and rose again from the grave. He is the source of all good things, and He offers something even greater than food, sex, or health. When we turn from our limited self-sufficiency and trust and turn to Christ, we find real, lasting peace. He offers an eternal life of joy and complete fulfillment for all who trust in Him."

Read Isaiah 64:6-7. How does God describe our good deeds apart from Christ?

Where do you see the sin of pride in your own life? Consider areas of pride or self-righteousness. Are there times you look down on others because they are not making the same lifestyle choices that you are (i.e., the type of food you buy, how often you do or do not work out, how much you have in your savings account, etc.).

How does the gospel speak to our pride?

"The gospel provides hope for us all."

For the One Who Longs to be Loved and Known

|

READ JOHN 4:1-42

"Give me the love that leads the way, the faith that nothing can dismay, the hope no disappointments tire, the passion that will burn like fire. Let me not sink to be a clod: make me Thy fuel, Flame of God."

AMY CARMICHAEL

We all want to be known and loved. We may even fear rejection from others, wondering, "If someone really knew me—the real me—would they still love me?"

As Christians, we have found an all-satisfying love in Christ, who knows us completely and loves us unconditionally. His love offers us true freedom, joy, and peace in the world. Even if others forsake us, or even when we fail, we have confidence that our good Father loves us. For our friends who do not yet know Christ, however, this desire still exists. Many of our friends seek this in relationships. Perhaps they look to their spouse to offer ultimate validation. Or maybe they become a serial dater, hopping from one boyfriend to the next. Perhaps they look for love through the men in their lives because their dad left when they were little. Or, maybe they come across as insecure and needy in relationships, always wanting more from you than you can give—more attention, more affirmation, more time.

The gospel provides hope for us all. If you identify the desire to be known and loved as a major theme in your friend's life, pray for them. Prayerfully seek an opportunity to share the hope of Christ with your friend. As you share about God's love for them, affirm your care and love for them as well. In this way, you can model the love of the Father in a tangible way.

COMMON GROUND

We all have a God-sized hole in our hearts that only God can fill. As you engage with your friend, think of a time when you looked to another person to fulfill you. Share how God's love and approval of you in Christ has changed your life.

A GOSPEL PRESENTATION TO ONE LONGING TO BE KNOWN AND LOVED

You may also be able to share the gospel by telling your friend a relevant Bible story. You could say something like, "I have been praying for you, and know you've been feeling down. Your story reminded me of another story, of a woman from many years ago who found true love. Can I share it with you?" Then share a story about God's love, such as this one from John 4:1-42:

Thousands of years ago, there was a woman who had been married five times. Given cultural marriage patterns and divorce rates, this woman would have been the source of one scandalous rumor after another. She knew that she was the talk of the town, so she kept to herself, likely protecting her heart from even more disappointment. Now, she was older, more experienced, and with a man who was not her husband.

One day, this woman went out to draw water from the well. Most women of the town would gather when the weather was cooler to talk and help one another in their tasks. But this woman went alone. We can guess that she did not want to see anyone. She likely felt bad enough as it was, filling the gnawing pain in her heart with one relationship after another. So she became a loner, drawing her water by herself in the heat of the day.

As she was following her usual routine, a man was sitting by the well and asked her for some water. He was a Jew, and she, a Samaritan, and in that time, the two did not mix. Jews thought Samaritans were dirty, half-breeds, and they would not even eat with them. So she responded to the man's request for water by saying, "You are a Jew, and I am a Samaritan. How can you ask me for a drink?" This man responded mysteriously, giving a puzzling answer about living water. He then proceeded to tell her all about her life, telling her about her many secrets and many husbands.

She was amazed! How could this man know all that she had done and still sit here talking with her? And she, a Samaritan woman, no less! The woman concluded that the man must be a prophet and told Him that she knew a Savior was coming. Jesus then told her, "I, the one speaking to you, am he."

This woman, who had been the source of shame in her town, was called out by Jesus, known fully by Him and loved completely. He knew what she was trying to hide. He knew everything she had ever done, and He still loved her. He saw it all, and He cherished her unconditionally. He pursued her in conversation and invited her to believe in Him.

This was so remarkable to the woman that she left her jar and told everyone in her town about Jesus. They came out to hear Him speak firsthand, and many were saved. Amazingly, God chose this lonely woman to save many in her town.

Sweet friend, God loves you just like He loved this woman. He knows you, down to the minuscule details of your life. He knows the things that you have done with excellence and the secrets you are trying to hide. He knows the number of hairs on your head and your deepest fears. He knows you completely, and He loves you with an all-satisfying, life-changing love. His love is better than anything. It is what we are all ultimately looking for, deep down.

His is a love that does not leave us in our sin but calls us to something better. When we repent and believe in His perfect life, death, and resurrection, we find what we are really looking for — the One who knows us and loves us completely. I would love for you to know the same kind of love and peace.

FOLLOW-UP QUESTIONS:

As you finish sharing, ask your friend a follow-up question like, *"What do you think about this story? Have you heard it before?"* Pray for your friend, and keep loving her, even if she does not respond in faith right away.

66

We all have a God-sized hole in our hearts that only God can fill.

What are some of the places people go for love?

_____

_____

_____

_____

_____

_____

_____

Why do we fear being both fully known and loved?

_____

_____

_____

_____

_____

_____

_____

Read Romans 5:6-8. How does Christ demonstrate His love for us? How do these verses remind us that we do not earn God's love, but it is a free and radical gift?

_____

_____

_____

_____

_____

_____

_____

As Christians,
we have found an
all-satisfying love in
Christ, who knows us
completely and loves
us unconditionally.

"*We are lovely because God loves us.*"

For the One Who is Searching for Significance

READ ROMANS 12:3-6, EPHESIANS 2:1-10

"These bold brothers and sisters weren't just willing to live for Jesus; they were willing to die for Him. I asked myself —as I have a thousand times since— why are so few of us in America willing to live for Jesus when others are so willing to die for Him? Seeing Jesus through the eyes of the persecuted church transformed me."

JOHNNIE MOORE

We all want to be important. We desire to be valuable, loved, and special. Perhaps we seek to fulfill this longing by climbing the corporate ladder or becoming the best in our field. Maybe we desperately desire to become a wife or mother and hope that these positions will bring the happiness that has eluded us thus far. Or, perhaps we endlessly strive to win the approval of everyone around us, resorting to putting others down to make ourselves look better.

The desire to be significant is a common one because we are significant. We are made in the image of God. Our lives have value, not because of what we do but because of who made us. For those of us who have trusted in Jesus as our Savior, we have found that ultimate significance and purpose are found only in God. We have found purpose as His child and have confidence in His love. We have been reconciled to our Maker and know that nothing can make God love us more or less.

For those who have not yet trusted in Christ, however, the search for significance can be an addicting and consuming path. There is always another dollar to earn, another person's approval to win, or another high to chase. There is always someone richer, smarter, or more beautiful. If you identify that your friend is searching for significance, this can be a great entry point to share the hope you have found in Christ.

COMMON GROUND

When you identify the quest for significance in your friends, seek to empathize and relate with them. We all want our lives to matter. We want to do good in the world and make a difference. However differently we each may define "success," we want to be successful. Perhaps we want to be a good mom or the CEO of a Fortune 500 company or to leave a legacy. As you relate with your friend, share an example from your own life. Recount a time when a quest for significance consumed your attention but left you disappointed.

THE PROBLEM

When the source of our significance is not eternal, it will always fail us. It cannot bear the weight of all our hopes and dreams. Our works are never enough, and our position will never be fully secure. We will never be smart enough, rich enough, or pretty enough to calm the underlying cravings and insecurities within our hearts. We can lose the money, our looks will fade, and a younger, more qualified person can always surpass us at work. We will all, from time to time, fail. If we place our worth on being successful, we will never be satisfied. Whenever we look to relationships or our jobs to provide ultimate significance, we will be disappointed.

Whatever we place as the ultimate authority in our lives becomes our god. We will sacrifice time, money, or our families to achieve its end. The desire to be significant is not wrong, but it is dangerous when that desire is rooted in something other than God. Like a bridge under a load it was never meant to carry, our foundations will inevitably crumble. Even a good thing, like the desire to be significant, will enslave us if we let it.

A GOSPEL PRESENTATION FOR ONE SEARCHING FOR SIGNIFICANCE

As we share the gospel with our friends who are searching for significance, we remember that there is only one kind of purpose that lasts forever. God, who made us, created us to know Him and enjoy Him forever. He is the source of all satisfaction and the giver of every good thing. He loves us and made us in His likeness. Our lives are of infinite worth, not because we have achieved great things in the world but because our Holy God made us. We have value, dignity, and significance because of the One who created us. And God gives His children a divine purpose—to join Him in His rescue mission of the world.

The problem is we rebelled against the design of the beautiful God who created us. We sought to find fulfillment apart from Him. We looked for ultimate significance in our work, relationships, or positions. And in doing so, we broke ties with the One who gives our lives meaning. We became helpless, traitors, and enemies of God. All the while, God was holding out His loving hands, patiently longing for us to return to Him.

Thankfully, God showed mercy on us and paved the way for our salvation by sending His Son, Jesus. When Jesus came, He lived a completely perfect life. He lived with purpose, peace, and joy, sinlessly obeying the Father's commands. He pointed us back to the source of life and fulfillment. He loved us so much that He died on a cross to pay for our sins, and then, three days after He died, He rose from the grave.

God did not love us because we were good enough to earn His favor. Rather, while we were still His enemies, Christ died for us. When we follow God, He not only saves us, He also makes us sons and daughters of the King. We are given significance and purpose, not only in this life but in the one to come.

One day, every person will die, and our work will die with us. But through Christ, there is a purpose that lasts forever—to be reunited with our King and worship Him forever.

daily QUESTIONS

How have you looked to the world to find significance?

Look at Ephesians 2:1-10. What does the Scripture say about the worth and significance we have in Christ?

Read Romans 12:3-6. How can you use your particular giftings to serve others?

"God gives His children a divine purpose—to join Him in His rescue mission of the world."

What's Next?
Follow-up and Discipleship

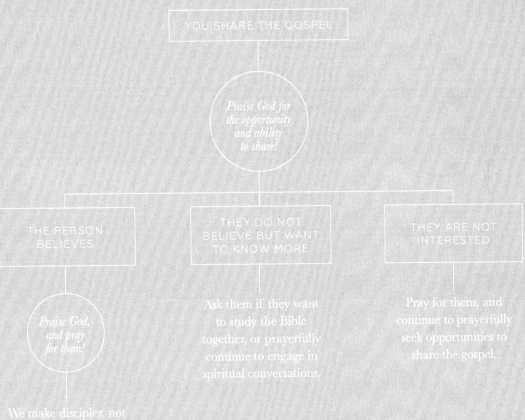

YOU SHARE THE GOSPEL

Praise God for the opportunity and ability to share!

THE PERSON BELIEVES

THEY DO NOT BELIEVE BUT WANT TO KNOW MORE

THEY ARE NOT INTERESTED

Praise God, and pray for them!

Ask them if they want to study the Bible together, or prayerfully continue to engage in spiritual conversations.

Pray for them, and continue to prayerfully seek opportunities to share the gospel.

We make disciples, not converts. So when someone believes, immediately get them connected with a local church. Start discipling them with gospel-centered discipleship material, such as The Daily Grace Co. study *Better Together: A Guide for Discipleship*.

World Religions

The following graphs show recent world religion statistics. According to a recent Pew survey, all major religions—except for Buddhism—are expected to increase by 2050. As seen in the graphs, Christianity is declining in America, while religious "nones" (no religious affiliation) are growing. Islam is the fastest-growing religion in the world, and it is predicted that by 2075, it will become the largest religion worldwide.

Even if you do not know a Muslim, Hindu, or Buddhist, take some time to read through the sections provided on other world religions so that you will feel better equipped for future conversations.

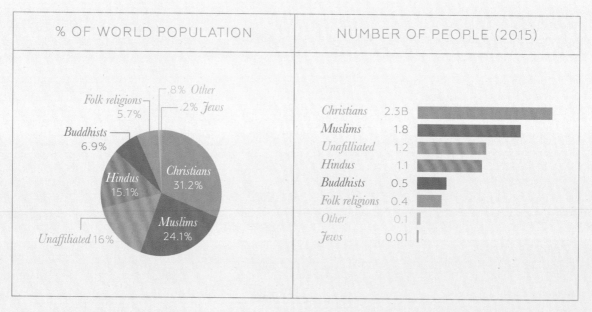

Source: Pew Research Center demographic projections. "The Changing Global Religious Landscape"
www.pewresearch.org | www.pewforum.org

DECLINE OF AMERICAN CHRISTIANITY & THE RISE OF THE RELIGIOUSLY UNAFILLIATED

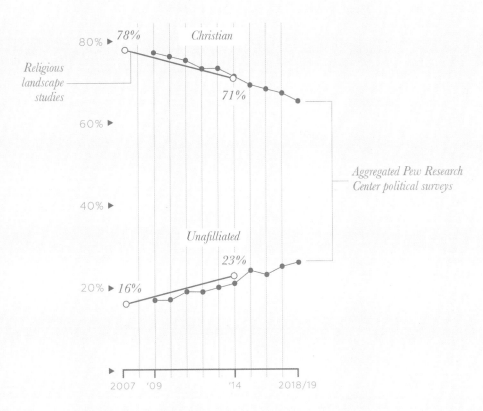

Source: Pew Research Center Religious Landscape studies (2007 and 2014).
Aggregated Pew Research Center political surveys conducted 2009-July 2019 on
the telephone "In the US, Decline of Christianity Continues at Rapid Pace"

www.pewresearch.org | www.pewforum.org

MUSLIMS PROJECTED TO BE FASTEST-GROWING MAJOR RELIGIOUS GROUP

Estimated percent change in population size, 2015-2060

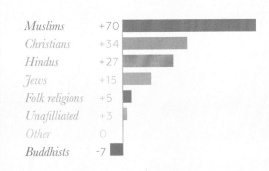

Muslims	+70
Christians	+34
Hindus	+27
Jews	+15
Folk religions	+5
Unafilliated	+3
Other	0
Buddhists	-7

Source: Pew Research Center demographic projections. "The Changing Global Religious Landscape"

www.pewresearch.org | www.pewforum.org

Islam

There are over 1.8 billion Muslims in the world today. Islam is currently the second-largest religion in the world, second only to Christianity. Islam is founded on the teachings of the Quran, a book which the prophet Mohammed claimed was given to him by the angel Gabriel in 610 AD. The word "Islam" means "submission," and Muslims believe in submission to one God, Allah. Just as in Christianity, there is a spectrum of beliefs within practicing Muslims. As you engage with a Muslim, do not make assumptions. Ask lots of questions, and be a good listener. Be prepared to share who Jesus is and how no person is good enough to earn God's favor. We all need a perfect sacrifice to cover our sins.

FIVE PILLARS

- *God: The belief that there is only one God.*

- *Prayer: Muslims pray five times a day facing Mecca where Mohammad claimed to have his vision from Gabriel.*

- *Alms: In accordance with Islamic law, Muslims give 2.5% of their wealth to the poor.*

- *Fasting: During the month of Ramadan, Muslims fast from sunrise to sunset.*

- *Pilgrimage: For Muslims who can afford to do so, Muslims are to travel to Mecca.*

THE QURAN

Believe in the Quran as their sacred text. They also believe that the Bible was distorted over time and that the Quran is the accurate interpretation of God's will.

- *Belief that there is one God who is holy and perfect. Many Muslims misunderstand the Christian concept of the Trinity, thinking that Christians believe in three gods.*

- *We are all sinners and need to be cleansed from our sin.*

- *Belief in many Old Testament people such as Adam, Abraham, Moses, and David.*

- *Belief in a judgment day and heaven and hell.*

- *Belief in the Torah, or the first five books of the Bible. Muslims believe that they are descendants of Abraham's son, Ishmael.*

- *Muslims have a desire to please God, pray, and pursue holiness.*

ENTRY QUESTIONS

- *You're a Muslim? Will you tell me about that?*

- *What are some of the things you believe as a Muslim?*

- *What is it like being a Muslim in _____?*
  (insert your city or country)

- *What do you base your truth on?*
  Do you have a holy book?

- *What do you think happens after you die?*

- *How do you get rid of your guilt or sin?*

- *What do you believe about Jesus?*

- *Cleansing is a big part of Muslim culture.*
  To enter a mosque, they must clean their hands and
  face. Ask about this and how they clean their hearts.

CONVERSATION TIPS

1. *Muslim culture highly values friendship.* As you seek to share the gospel, be a good friend. Do not attack your friend for his or her beliefs, but listen well, and engage with grace. Use your testimony to personally share about God's grace in your life while also sharing about His holiness.

2. *Muslims believe in a holy book and that Jesus was a prophet.* If your friend is willing, invite them to study the Scriptures with you to learn more about Isa al-Masih (Jesus's name in Arabic). Many Muslims believe that the Bible was distorted by humans throughout the years and that the Quran is the only criterion by which the Bible's accuracy can be judged. Refer back to week four, day one for more information on Biblical accuracy and authority.

3. *In Islam, sacrifices are commonly understood.* As you share the gospel, share the metanarrative of Scripture, using sacrifices as a common theme. For example, you might say something like, "Because of their sin, Adam and Eve were ashamed and naked. They were separated from God. Though there was a punishment for their sin, and they were cast out of the garden, God still loved them. He killed an animal to cover their nakedness, which was the first sacrifice. Throughout the years, Adam's descendants kept sinning and offering sacrifices, but it was never enough. Their sin was too great. But God loved His people and wanted to make a way for their sins to be forgiven. When Jesus came, He came as the perfect sacrifice. He was fully God and fully man. He lived a perfect life, died on the cross, and rose from the dead. He promises that whoever believes in Him will have their sins forgiven. He will offer them His perfection and cleanse them of their guilt."

4. *If you ask a Muslim if they go to heaven after they die, they will say, "Insha'Allah" or "If Allah wills it."* They have no assurance of their salvation, even if they live nearly perfect lives. Some Muslims use the analogy of a man walking on a small bridge from this life to the next. This bridge is called As-Sirāt, and it is as thin as a hair, but sharp as a knife (Islamic hadith). If they have done too many bad deeds, they will fall off the bridge into hell, but no one knows if they will be saved until the moment of judgment. As you share your testimony, share the assurance of salvation you have because of Jesus's perfection.

5. *For many, Isalm is not only a personal belief but is also tied into their family culture.* For them to reject Islam could mean a rejection from their family or town. Be bold in sharing the gospel, but also be sensitive to what it would cost your friend to follow Jesus.

66

Be prepared to share who Jesus is and how no person is good enough to earn God's favor.

Hinduism

Hinduism is the third largest religion in the world. There are over one billion Hindus worldwide. Hindus historically believe that there are many gods and goddesses, but they only worship a single deity called "Brahman." They also believe that salvation comes breaking free from death and reincarnation. Just a there are many denominations in Christianity, each Hindu's belief system may differ from pure doctrine. As you engage with a Hindu, ask questions and listen well. Be prepared to share Bible stories and pray.

CORE BELIEFS

- *Strong values of moral virtue and karma*
  - *Dharma: this is their moral law for individual conduct.*
  - *Karma: what a person does affects what happens to them in life.*
- *Combination of several holy texts known as the Vedas.*
- *At one level, Hindus believe that god is one. Yet Hinduism also has thousands of gods, and many believe there are multiple ways to get to god. Hindu gods can be good or bad.*

- *Devotion is an important aspect of Hinduism, and families might have a family god, or individuals may have an individual god.*
- *Belief in reincarnation. Souls have eternal lives.*
- *Worship in temples or shrines in their homes. They often offer gifts such as fruit or flowers to the altar for prosperity and favor.*
- *Salvation is breaking free from the cycle of rebirth, achieved by perfected works, knowledge, or devotion.*

COMMON GROUND

- *Value spirituality and morality.*
- *Belief that Jesus really existed—some Hindus believe that He was one manifestation of a god.*

- *Desire for salvation.*
- *Desire to please and be devoted to a god.*

Hinduism

ENTRY QUESTIONS

- *You are Hindu? Will you tell me about that?*

- *What are some of the things you believe as a Hindu?*

- *What is it like being a Hindu in _____?*
  (insert your city or country)

- *On what do you base your truth? Do you have a holy book?*

- *What do you think happens after you die?*

- *What do you believe about Jesus?*

CONVERSATION TIPS

1. *Hindus believe that there are many gods who have different powers.* As you share the gospel, make sure to clarify that the God we are talking about is the all-powerful, good God—God Most High. One way to do this is by Bible storying. Do not be afraid of the supernatural stories of Jesus. Telling stories about Jesus can be a really effective way to share the gospel with Hindus.

2. *Hindus believe in holy books,* so as you are sharing, include that these stories are found in the Holy Bible, a book given by God, and that all its words are completely true.

3. *In traditional Hindu belief, people die and come to life often.* This is the belief of reincarnation. As you discuss the resurrection, share how Jesus's coming to life again was different. He came in the same body, with scars on His hands to prove that He was the same man.

4. *While Hindus give fruit offerings to obtain blessings, God has blessed us even though we do not deserve it.* We can notice that Hindus must make sacrifices or offer gifts to win their gods' favor, while Jesus paid the once-and-for-all offering for those who believe in Him. When we believe in Jesus, we are saved and set free from sin and are given eternal life with God in heaven.

Buddhism

There are over 500 million people who adhere to the teachings of Buddha, with the greatest quantity living in China, India, and the United States. Buddhism's genesis story begins with a prince named Siddhartha Gautama who left his palace in the 6th century BC. After leaving his palace, he saw four men—one sick, one old, one dead, and one monk. He realized through this encounter that not even a prince can escape suffering and death. He spent many years trying to understand the purpose of suffering and sought truth through deep meditation. This man was eventually given the title of Buddha, or Enlightened One. As we share the gospel with Buddists, remember to be kind and gentle, sharing the truth with grace and truth.

THREE UNIVERSAL TRUTHS

- *Everything is impermanent and constantly changing.*

- *Because nothing is permanent in life, all who live suffer.*

- *"Self" does not exist.*

FOUR NOBLE TRUTHS

- *Life is full of suffering.*

- *Suffering is caused by desire, attachment, and greed.*

- *Suffering can be overcome.*

- *The way to overcome desire and suffering is through the Noble Eightfold, which leads to nirvana.*

THE EIGHTFOLD PATH: PRACTICES THAT LEAD TO NIRVANA:

- *Right seeing*

- *Right intention*

- *Right speech*

- *Right action*

- *Right work*

- *Right effort*

- *Right mindfulness*

- *Right concentration*

Buddhism

- *Understanding of the problem of suffering.*

- *Belief that possessions will not ultimately satisfy.*

- *Believe that suffering will one day end.*

- *The desire to live honest, decent lives.*

- *You are Buddhist? Will you tell me about that?*

- *What are some of the things you believe as a Buddhist?*

- *What is it like being a Buddhist in _____?*
  (insert your city or country)

- *On what do you base your truth?*
  Do you have a holy book?

- *Where do you think suffering comes from?*

- *What do you think happens after you die?*

- *What do you believe about Jesus?*

1. *Buddhists believe in karma, or the idea that actions lead to future consequences.* As you share, try to use this concept to help explain what Christ did in His perfect life, death, and resurrection. For example, you might ask, "If someone were to transfer all of their good karma to you out of love, how would you respond?"

2. *Use the information from week four, day three, for more information on a theology of suffering.* You may ask a question like, "If there was a God, do you think He could willingly suffer alongside us?"

3. *One main goal of Buddhists is to rid themselves of desire.* Ask your friend how it is possible to do this. Are not some desires good?

4. *Buddhists' ultimate goal is to achieve a state of non-existence.* Ask your friend how he or she feels about this future state.

5. *Buddhists believe that they can become good enough to rid themselves of their guilt.* Ask more questions about how they rid themselves of guilt when they fail and how they think they will eventually succeed.

"Remember to
be kind and gentle,
sharing the truth
with grace and truth."

But in your hearts
regard Christ the Lord
as holy, ready at any
time to give a defense
to anyone who asks you
for a reason for the
hope that is in you.

1 PETER 3:15

weekly REFLECTION

Review all Scripture passages from the week.

Summarize the main points from this week's Scripture readings.

What did you observe from this week's passages about God and His character?

What do this week's passages reveal about the condition of mankind and yourself?

How do these passages point to the gospel?

How should you respond to these Scriptures? What specific action steps can you take this week to apply them in your life?

Write a prayer in response to your study of God's Word. Adore God for who He is, confess sins He revealed in your own life, ask Him to empower you to walk in obedience, and pray for anyone who comes to mind as you study.

A Closing Prayer

Lord, You are worthy.
One day, every tongue will proclaim that You are Lord!
Until then, we want to joyfully bring others to Your throne.
Having tasted Your goodness firsthand,
we want to now lead others to the fountain of life.

Lord, when we are preoccupied with ourselves,
so afraid of what our friends think of us—
giving them a perceived power over our lives,
and when we forget the nature of forever,
distracted with the incessant shouting of temporal
distractions, bring clarity.
Convict us. Burden us.
And lead us to repentance.

Show us what truly matters: the eternal souls of the
friends and family that surround us every day.
Open our eyes to have Your heart for the lost,
for the hurting, for the bitter and broken.
When we see the weight of sin yanking our friends
to the depth of the ocean,
may we not be silent.
Let us not be so deceived, selfish, or
stuck in fear so as to do nothing,
when in fact, the moments are so limited.
We are not guaranteed another day,
yet alone another breath.
May we use every second of our lives for Your glory.

When we face the brokenness of the day,
let us respond with hope and love, as You did.
Burden us for the lost.
Give us entry points to share the gospel and
the courage to take them.

Give us an eagerness to share the hope that
was once shared with us.
Grant us wisdom, courage, tact,
passion, and clarity.
As we gaze at Your eternal face, let us be emboldened
to be emissaries of Your reconciling message.

Give us humility to remember that
we cannot change hearts.
And give us dependence on You as our judge and Savior.

Oh Lord, bring salvation to our neighbors, friends,
co-workers, and family.
May we be little children who constantly intercede
to our great Father,
asking You to do what You do best—to make
all things right.
We long for others to know You.
We want Your name lifted high.

Show us how to do this, we pray.

What is the Gospel ?

THANK YOU FOR READING AND ENJOYING THIS STUDY WITH US! WE ARE ABUNDANTLY GRATEFUL FOR THE WORD OF GOD, THE INSTRUCTION WE GLEAN FROM IT, AND THE EVER-GROWING UNDERSTANDING IT PROVIDES FOR US OF GOD'S CHARACTER. WE ARE ALSO THANKFUL THAT SCRIPTURE CONTINUALLY POINTS TO ONE THING IN INNUMERABLE WAYS: THE GOSPEL.

We remember our brokenness when we read about the fall of Adam and Eve in the garden of Eden (Genesis 3), where sin entered into a perfect world and maimed it. We remember the necessity that something innocent must die to pay for our sin when we read about the atoning sacrifices in the Old Testament. We read that we have all sinned and fallen short of the glory of God (Romans 3:23) and that the penalty for our brokenness, the wages of our sin, is death (Romans 6:23). We all need grace and mercy, but most importantly, we all need a Savior.

We consider the goodness of God when we realize that He did not plan to leave us in this dire state. We see His promise to buy us back from the clutches of sin and death in Genesis 3:15. And we see that promise accomplished with Jesus Christ on the cross. Jesus Christ knew no sin yet became sin so that we might become righteous through His sacrifice (2 Corinthians 5:21). Jesus was tempted in every way that we are and lived sinlessly. He was reviled yet still yielded Himself for our sake, that we may have life abundant in Him. Jesus lived the perfect life that we could not live and died the death that we deserved.

The gospel is profound yet simple. There are many mysteries in it that we will never understand this side of heaven, but there is still overwhelming weight to its implications in this life. The gospel tells of our sinfulness and God's goodness and a gracious gift that compels a response. We are saved by grace through faith, which means that we rest with faith in the grace that Jesus Christ displayed on the cross (Ephesians 2:8-9). We cannot save ourselves from our brokenness or do any amount of good works to merit God's favor. Still, we can have faith that what Jesus accomplished in His death, burial, and resurrection was more than enough for our salvation and our eternal delight. When we accept God, we are commanded to die to ourselves and our sinful desires and live a life worthy of the calling we have received (Ephesians 4:1). The gospel compels us to be sanctified, and in so doing, we are conformed to the likeness of Christ Himself. This is hope. This is redemption. This is the gospel.

SCRIPTURES TO REFERENCE:

GENESIS 3:15   I will put hostility between you and the woman, and between your offspring
                    and her offspring. He will strike your head, and you will strike his heel.

ROMANS 3:23   For all have sinned and fall short of the glory of God.

ROMANS 6:23   For the wages of sin is death, but the gift of God is eternal life in
                    Christ Jesus our Lord.

2 CORINTHIANS 5:21 He made the one who did not know sin to be sin for us, so that in him
                    we might become the righteousness of God.

EPHESIANS 2:8-9   For you are saved by grace through faith, and this is not from yourselves;
                    it is God's gift — not from works, so that no one can boast.

EPHESIANS 4:1-3   Therefore I, the prisoner in the Lord, urge you to walk worthy of
                    the calling you have received, with all humility and gentleness, with patience,
                    bearing with one another in love, making every effort to keep the unity of the
                    Spirit through the bond of peace.

Thank you for studying
God's Word with us!

CONNECT WITH US

@thedailygraceco
@dailygracepodcast
@kristinschmucker

CONTACT US

info@thedailygraceco.com

SHARE

#thedailygraceco
#lampandlight

VISIT US ONLINE

www.thedailygraceco.com

MORE DAILY GRACE

The Daily Grace App
Daily Grace Podcast